LANDSCAPED PARKS AND GARDENS OF EAST YORKSHIRE 1700-1830

DAVID NEAVE and DEBORAH TURNBULL

GEORGIAN SOCIETY FOR EAST YORKSHIRE

1992

ISBN 0 9513966 17

Front cover: Scampston Hall *c.*1780 by Francis Nicholson
York Minster Library (Reproduced by kind
permission of the Dean and Chapter of York)

Printed by Clifford Ward & Co. (Bridlington) Ltd.

INTRODUCTION

The landscape of East Yorkshire was transformed in the Georgian period largely through the actions of the landed gentry. It was they who instigated the enclosing of the open arable fields, sheep walks, rabbit warrens and waterlogged commons, and it was they who largely paid for the building of the new tiled farmsteads, the laying out of the roads and the planting of the hedgerows and woodland. Alongside their transformation of the wider landscape the landed gentry also transformed their more immediate environs by the laying out of gardens and parks in the fashionable natural style. The parkland thus created and the associated plantations are amongst the principal glories of the too often under appreciated landscape of the region.

East Yorkshire is not rich in landscaped parks, except in the north-west of the riding and along the western edge of the wolds, but the parks and gardens that it has illustrate well the history of landscape gardening in the eighteenth and nineteenth century. There are at Heslington, Londesborough, and Risby remnants of late seventeenth century gardens, at South Dalton a splendid Rococo survival, at Houghton, Rise, Scampston, and Sledmere perfect examples of the natural style and at Thorpe Hall, Rudston and Everingham essays in the picturesque. The East Riding can lay claim to three important figures in the history of landscape gardening, Richard 3rd Earl of Burlington, William Kent and William Mason. The last two were born in the county but no local landscape can be directly attributed to them. The leading designers Charles Bridgeman and Capability Brown did work here, the latter being responsible for five East Riding landscape parks. Brown's former foreman Thomas White 'improved' or provided 'improvement plans' for some eight estates and it was in the East Riding that he laid the foundations of his long successful career as a landscape gardener and arboriculturist. In the early-mid eighteenth century the celebrated Thomas Knowlton of Londesborough was the leading figure in gardening locally.

This study is an historical rather than a descriptive account of the landscaped parks of the East Riding of Yorkshire and the selection of those to be included in the gazetteer has been determined by the existence of plans and other relevant documentary material. For this reason a number of grounds well worth closer examination, such as those at Moreby, Place Newton, Settrington, Warter, and Winestead have been excluded and therefore this should not be considered a comprehensive account. An introductory essay on landscape gardening in the East Riding is followed by an illustrated gazetteer.

(from H. and J. A. Repton *Fragments on the Theory and Practice of Landscape Gardening*, 1816)

LANDSCAPE GARDENING IN EAST YORKSHIRE

The earliest description of a country house garden in the East Riding of Yorkshire is provided by Celia Fiennes who in 1697 paid a visit to her relative Sir Griffith Boynton at Burton Agnes Hall, near Bridlington. She observed that

> *the Gardens are large and are capable of being made very fine, they now remaine in the old fashion; there is one walke all the length of the Garden called the Crooked Walke, of grass well cutt and rowled, it is indented in and out in corners and so is the wall, which makes you thinke you are at the end of the walke severall tymes before you are, by means of the Codling hedge that is on the other side, this leads you to a Summer house that also opens to a large gravell walke that runns the breadth of the Garden to the house ward.*

Heslington Hall around 1900 (Hull University Photographic Service)

Around the courtyard between the hall and the gatehouse was 'cut box and filleroy and lawrell' and in the centre of the court 'a Bowling green palisado'd around'.[1] This old fashioned garden was no doubt contemporary with the house built at the beginning of the seventeenth century.

By the date of Celia Fiennes' visit to Burton Agnes a number of other East Riding country houses had been provided with more fashionable settings and were surrounded by formal gardens in the prevailing French or Dutch style. The finest gardens were at LONDESBOROUGH* where in the late 1670s a garden was laid out for the 1st Earl and Countess of Burlington to the designs of the scientist and architect Robert Hooke. Here were avenues, terraced walks, a fountain garden with statuary, parterres, a bowling green, a kitchen garden and formal plantations. Also formal but on a lesser scale were the gardens at HOWSHAM and RISBY. The latter were laid out in the 1680s for Sir James Bradshaw with Italianate terraces on the side of a valley, and although the house was demolished 200 years ago the earthworks of the gardens remain clearly visible in the landscape.

[*Names in capitals denote a separate entry in the gazetteer or biographical appendix]

At Heslington at the end of the seventeenth century, or early in the eighteenth century, James Yarborough created a modest garden in the Dutch style. A painting of the hall in 1760 shows a terrace with an avenue of yew trees leading to a tall garden pavilion overlooking a formal canal which extends into the park at a right angle to the terrace walk. The scene is very similar to the Dutch style canal garden at Westbury Court, Gloucestershire. The canal at Heslington has been replaced by an irregular lake but the pavilion remains and the yew trees, now clipped, have grown to an enormous size, providing the best example of topiary work in East

Yorkshire. This modest garden contrasts with the great dramatic landscapes at Castle Howard, Blenheim and Stowe with which James Yarborough's son-in-law Sir John Vanbrugh, the dramatist and architect, was associated.

At Blenheim, Stowe and elsewhere Vanburgh worked in conjunction with CHARLES BRIDGEMAN (c.1680-1738) who in 1728 was appointed Master Gardener to George II and was responsible among other things for the Round Pond and the Serpentine in Kensington Gardens. He created ambitious gardens in a transitional version of the formal French style. They were regular in form but with asymmetrical features and took into account the garden's natural setting. It was Bridgeman who introduced the ha-ha, or sunken fence, from France and considerably developed its use. He carried out one commission in the East Riding at SCAMPSTON for Sir William St. Quintin c.1730. Bridgeman's fine series of plans for Scampston, now in the Gough Collection, at the Bodleian Library, show an elaborate formal layout with a complicated water system.

Heslington Hall 1992. The summer house is on the right with the line of the former canal clearly visible in the foreground.

WHereas the Gardens of Charles Yarburgh, of Heſlington, Eſq; have been robb'd, three ſeveral Times, of Flower Roots, &c. to a conſiderable Value; the laſt Time of which was about the 7th or 8th Inſtant: Whoever will give Information of the Perſon or Perſons concern'd in any of the above Robberies, they ſhall receive Ten Guineas Reward.

York Courant 15 July 1755

Ha-Ha (based on engraving in H. and J. A. Repton, Fragments on the Theory and Practice of Landscape Gardening, *1816)*

Bridgeman also worked for the East Riding's foremost landowner, Richard, 3rd Earl of Burlington (1694-1753), but seemingly only at Chiswick c.1716. Burlington himself is considered an influential figure in the history of landscape gardening largely on the basis of the garden he created for his Palladian villa at Chiswick and the influence he had on his protégé William Kent (1685-1748). Kent, who was born at Bridlington worked as an historical painter in Italy before becoming a successful architect under Burlington's initial patronage.[2] It was through designing garden buildings that Kent's interest seemingly turned to garden design itself c.1730. Horace Walpole considered Kent to be 'the father of modern gardening':

> *He leaped the fence and saw that all nature was a garden. He felt the delicious contrast of hill and valley changing imperceptibly into each other, tasted the beauty of the gentle swell, or concave scoop, and remarked how loose groves crowned an easy eminence with happy ornament ... But of all the beauties that he added to the face of this beautiful country, none surpassed his management of water. Adieu to canals, circular basons and cascades tumbling down marble steps, the last absurd magnificence of Italian and French villas ... The gentle stream was taught to serpentise seemingly at its pleasure ... Its borders were smoothed, but preserved their waving irregularity.*[3]

Both Kent and Burlington thought of themselves as the introducers of the natural style and the role of the latter should not be overlooked.[4] Burlington in turn was influenced by his friend the poet Alexander Pope. Pope's famous directive to the landscape gardener to 'Consult the Genius of the place in all' comes from his epistle 'On Taste' which was dedicated to Lord Burlington and includes the following lines:

> *To build, to plant, whatever you intend,*
> *To rear the Column, or the Arch to bend,*
> *To swell the Terras, or to sink the Grot,*
> *In all, let Nature never be forgot.*[5]

Kent put into practice this advice and at Stowe, Rousham and to a lesser extent Chiswick he remodelled the regular layouts of his predecessor and introduced the natural style.

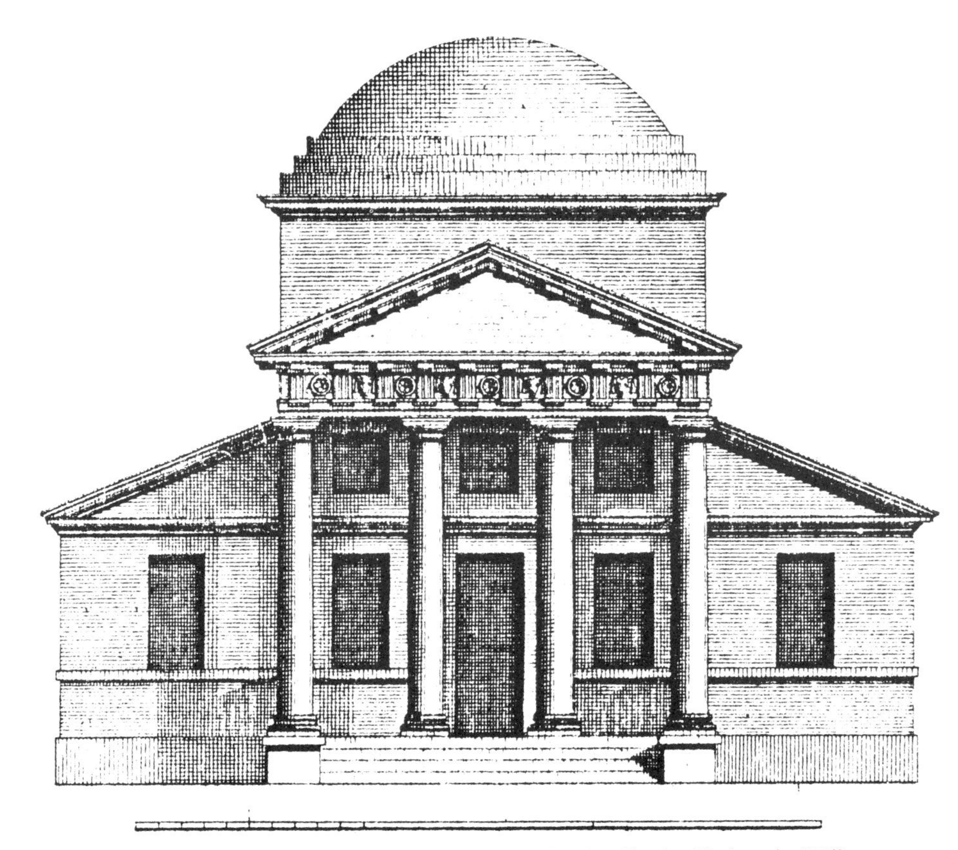

South Dalton, design for a temple or garden seat for Sir Charles Hotham by William Kent around 1730

No landscape garden in his native East Yorkshire can be attributed to William Kent but he is known to have stayed at LONDESBOROUGH with Lord Burlington during the time that extensive work was underway in the park and pleasure gardens. The grounds with their winding walks, irregular lakes and clumps of trees bear many of Kent's hallmarks and are a prime example of a landscape in transition from the formal to the natural style.

Kent did design a temple, which was not built, for Sir Charles Hotham's garden at SOUTH DALTON. This important Rococo garden, created in the 1730's, with its straight allee flanked by winding walks has similarities to the pleasure garden at Londesborough and it is known that Thomas Knowlton, Lord Burlington's gardener, gave advice on its design in 1729.

THOMAS KNOWLTON (1691-1781) who has been described as 'undoubtedly one of the most outstanding gardeners of his time' was at Londesborough from 1726 until his death 55 years later.[6] His great love was botany and he had a collection of rare and exotic plants in the hot houses in the kitchen garden. Although not primarily a landscape designer many local landowners sought his advice on the layout and planting of their grounds. He worked at BIRDSALL, BURTON CONSTABLE, EVERINGHAM, KILNWICK and SOUTH DALTON, in the East Riding, at Aldby Park, Duncombe Park and Swinton in the North Riding, and at Blyborough in Lincolnshire.

Knowlton was a friend of Stephen Switzer (1682-1745), nurseryman, seedsman and garden designer, the author of *The practical husbandman and planter* 1733-4 to which he subscribed. Switzer provided trees for the garden at South Dalton and he has been suggested as the designer of the remarkable water-garden at Ebberston Hall, North Riding a property that was inherited by the Hothams later in the century. Switzer did provide an elaborate scheme for the grounds of Nostell Priory, West Riding, a house designed by James Moyser (d.1753) of Beverley whose mother was the widow of Sir John Hotham, 3rd baronet.[7]

Thomas Knowlton's tomb, 1781, in Londesborough churchyard (*Hull University Photographic Service*)

Moyser and his father, John (d.1738) along with Sir Charles Hotham (d.1738), 5th baronet and his cousin Col. James Gee (1686-1751) of Bishop Burton were the principal members of Burlington's circle in the East Riding. They frequently shared his table at Londesborough and ideas on gardening must have been discussed. The Moysers lived in North Bar Within, Beverley in a predecessor of St. Mary's Manor. In 1724 an anonymous visitor described the Moysers' beautiful gardens 'which in four acres of ground contain a great variety of avenues of firs, of parterre, of statues; and also of arbours, seats and vases in trilliage work; besides two seats one of Ionic pilaster, the other of Doric pillars painted by Parmentier'.[8] This garden was not yet affected by the natural style but a description in 1754-5 of the grounds of James Gee's house, Low Hall, Bishop Burton, for which Burlington provided designs, suggests that they were less formal. As well as a two-acre walled garden 'well planted with fruit trees' there was an agreeable 'Wilderness or young wood disposed into walks, of about five acres, adjoining the house'.[9]

William Kent died in 1748 and his position as the leading garden designer was taken in the 1750s by LANCELOT BROWN (1715-83), head gardener at Stowe 1741-51. Brown who earned the nickname 'Capability' by 1760 was undoubtedly the most prolific landscape gardener of all time and his achievements in the development of the natural style are too well known to need elaboration.[10] Out of the 200 or more commissions he received five were for schemes for the improvement of landscapes in the East Riding at BURTON CONSTABLE, HOWSHAM, RISE, SCAMPSTON and SLEDMERE. Each was implemented to a lesser or greater extent. At Burton Constable and Sledmere improvement plans were also provided by Brown's former assistant THOMAS WHITE (1739-1811) of West Retford, Nottinghamshire, then Lanchester, County Durham, who was to become the most active landscape gardener in the north of England and Scotland in the later eighteenth and early nineteenth century.[11]

White acted as foreman for Capability Brown at a number of places including Sandbeck and Temple Newsam in the years 1759-65. Some of his earliest independent commissions were in the East Riding at BURTON CONSTABLE (1768), HOUGHTON (1768), and WELTON (1769). He was back in the Riding from the mid-1770s providing plans for SLEDMERE (1776) and HOLME-ON-SPALDING MOOR (1777) and advising on the landscaping at GRIMSTON GARTH (1782). He may also have designed the landscape at KILNWICK-ON-THE-WOLDS. Payments into his bank account indicate work for Henry Vavasour at Melbourne Hall (1793-4) and possibly at BIRDSALL for Henry

*Title from Adam Mickle's plan for the grounds of Walkington Lodge 1803 (*by permission of Hull University Archivist*)*

Willoughby (1776-7). He also provided an improvement plan in 1775 for Sir Robert Darcy Hildyard of Winestead (Red Hall) but this would seem to have been for his North Riding seat at Sedbury. White's landscapes echoed those of Brown and were characterised by perimeter plantations, clumps of trees and where possible a serpentine lake. He produced delightful coloured plans and for this reason many have survived, some still gracing the walls of the homes of the descendants of his patrons.

Brown and White did not get all the East Riding commissions in the 'age of improvement'. WILLIAM EMES (1730-1803), who chiefly worked in the Midlands and Wales, was responsible for the landscaping of CAVE CASTLE, SOUTH CAVE in 1787 and in 1803 ADAM MICKLE (d.1809), of Bedale, provided a plan for the grounds of Walkington Lodge which had been built by the Beverley solicitor John Lockwood.[12] The somewhat old-fashioned scheme which contained the classical Brownian features of lawn areas, clumps, single trees and perimeter plantations was for a greater area than was then owned by Lockwood and was seemingly not implemented.

The great activity on the part of East Riding landowners in laying out their grounds from the mid 1760s was closely linked to agricultural improvement and the enclosure movement. In some cases the grounds around the country houses were hemmed in by open arable fields, village housing and public roads and without Parliamentary enclosure the laying out of 'suitable' grounds would have been impossible. At NORTH CAVE, EVERINGHAM, HOTHAM, WELTON, HOLME-ON-SPALDING MOOR, SLEDMERE, SOUTH CAVE, and Melbourne enclosure of the open fields immediately preceded landscaping. Public roads were diverted away from the hall or proposed parkland under the enclosure act or by an order from Quarter Sessions as occurred at BIRDSALL, BOYNTON, ESCRICK (twice), EVERINGHAM, NORTH and SOUTH CAVE, RISE, SCAMPSTON and WELTON.

Removing housing could be more difficult but the total, or partial, removal of villages for emparking is a common theme in 18th century landscape history, highlighted by Oliver Goldsmith in his poem *The Deserted Village* (1770) and a number of East Riding examples can be cited. When the park at LONDESBOROUGH was enlarged in 1739 the hamlet of Easthorpe was virtually destroyed. At HOWSHAM Nathaniel Cholmley removed more than half the village in two stages when creating his park c.1755-75. All the village houses of the large village of SLEDMERE were demolished by Sir Christopher Sykes and only a handful of buildings were initially erected outside the park to replace them. At ESCRICK as well as removing a major part of the village Beilby Thompson obtained an Act of Parliament in 1781 to demolish the church and rectory and rebuild them on a new site to the north. Village houses were also removed at BIRDSALL in the 18th century and here too in 1822 the village church was rebuilt on the edge of the park leaving the old church alongside the house as a picturesque ruin.

Wassand, the thatched cottage on an island in Hornsea Mere, from a mid-nineteenth century watercolour
(Georgian Society for East Yorkshire)

The enthusiasm for the improvement of country house grounds seems to have declined in the East Riding during the Napoleonic Wars and Humphry Repton (1752-1818), the leading exponent at that time was never employed in the area. Local landscaping activity was resumed in 1815 with the digging of the Upper Pond at THORPE HALL, RUDSTON, the first stage in the creation of its fine picturesque grounds with denser planting, irregular linked lakes and a charming group of garden buildings. At the same period the Revd. Charles Constable began the planting and building at Wassand which produced a similar picturesque landscape incorporating the large Hornsea Mere. Around this estate were placed a series of rustic buildings, including a thatched Tea House built in 1818 on one of the islands in the Mere.[13].

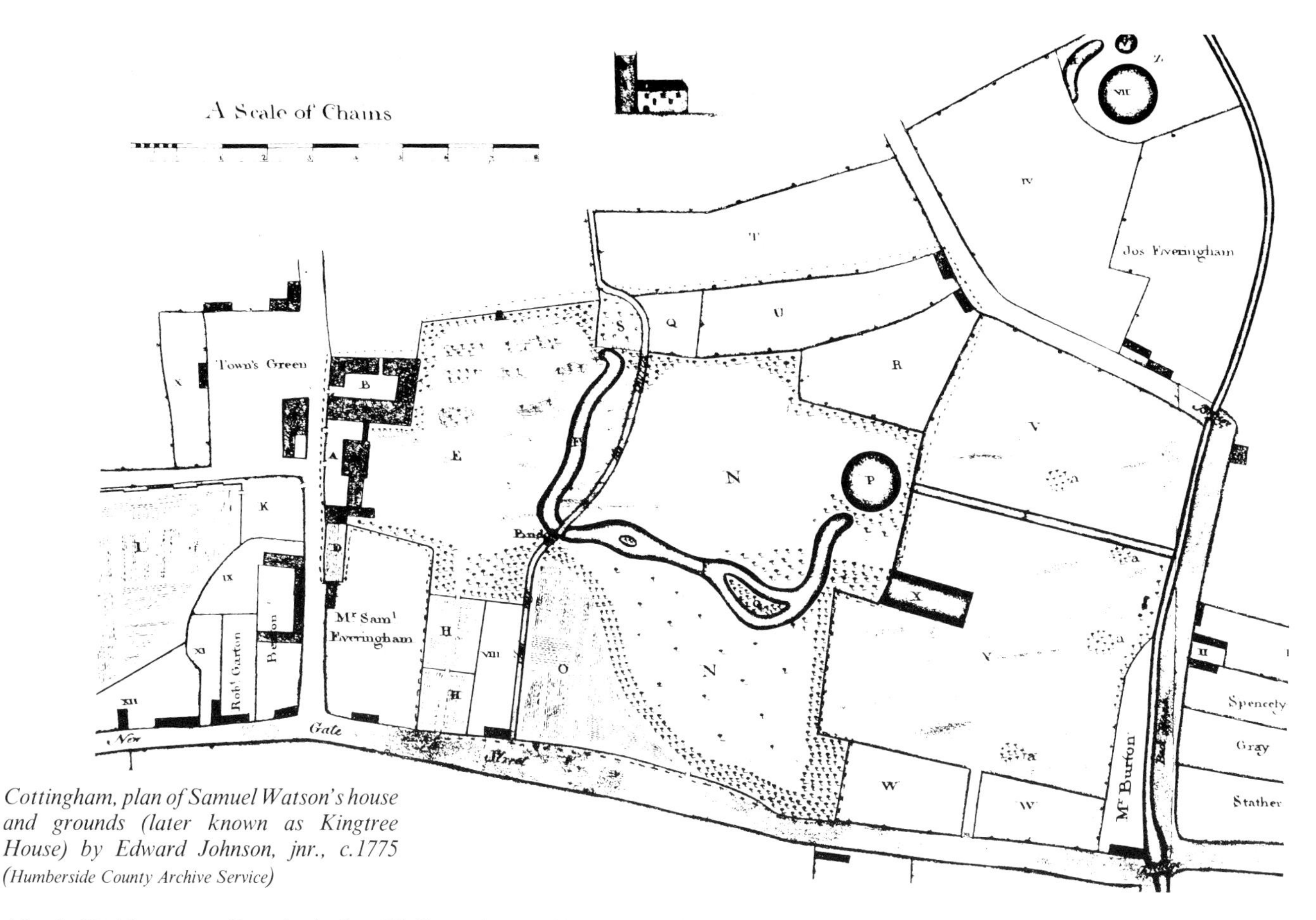

Cottingham, plan of Samuel Watson's house and grounds (later known as Kingtree House) by Edward Johnson, jnr., c.1775
(Humberside County Archive Service)

Also in Holderness at Benningholme Hall the extensive grounds were 'tastefully laid-out'. There was a 'fine avenue ... about two miles in length; also a splendid fish pond, or small lake, containing two picturesque islands' on one of which there was 'a very neat temple ... and a very neat Grotto in the grounds'.[14] No landscape designer has been identified with these schemes, nor with the contemporary work at ESCRICK, RISE, and HOTHAM HALL. In the case of EVERINGHAM the improvements carried out for William Constable-Maxwell in 1826-7 were supervised by the little known landscape gardener J. N. Sleed of Kensington, a follower of the great writer on gardening and garden design, John Claudius Loudon (1783-1843).

Loudon directed much that he wrote at the urban middle class and their suburban villas rather than at the great landowners and their country estates. It was the age of the villa garden. The landscaping of the modest grounds of merchant villas was not a new phenomenon and a number of 18th century East Riding examples can be given including WELTON HOUSE where White provided a plan for the Hull merchant Thomas Williamson in 1769. This garden has now gone as have those of most of the other 'elegant and thick-sown' villas which from the later 18th century adorned the villages to the west of Hull and which in Anna Seward's words made the whole country seem 'an extended range of pleasure-grounds, so richly has it been cultivated and adorned by mercantile opulence'.[15] At Cottingham in 1769 the agricultural writer Arthur Young saw the grounds of the Hull merchant Samuel Watson at Kingtree House and described them at some length. He thought the pleasure ground 'very well worth seeing

> *it consists of shrubberies with winding walks, and the imitation of a meandering river through the whole. The grass plot in front of the house surrounded with ever-greens and shrubs, with a Gothic bench on one side, is very pretty, and the clumps to the water's edge well disposed ...*[16]

Kingtree House has been demolished and the grounds built upon but nearby at Thwaite Hall a splendid villa garden, laid out in the early 19th century for the Hull merchant and shipowner John Hentig, fortunately survives. It covers some 30 acres and has a large irregular lake created later in the 19th century from a more regular fishpond. Also to the west of Cottingham in the grounds of Castle Hill Hospital can be seen a castellated folly, the surviving remnant of the house and grounds of another Hull merchant, Thomas Thompson (1754-1828). The tower was built in 1825 in the grounds of the recently completed Cottingham Castle as a lookout for viewing 'the Humber and the lovely land on every side'. Inside, at the top there was to be a table with a map identifying all the places which could be seen, and 'suitable extracts from our best poets' including Cowper and Goldsmith.[17]

Everywhere in the early nineteenth century the grounds of more modest houses were being laid out and adorned with buildings and artificial ruins. At Hedon in the grounds of Ivy House, the attorney James Iveson gathered together medieval stonework and erected a 'Tomb' or mausoleum, c.1820, on the mythical site of the burial place of 'Lady Albina' the murdered wife of Drogo de la Beuvriere, the first Lord of Holderness.[18] Around 1800 Robert Leighton, a Market Weighton merchant, created a pleasure garden on land at Goodmanham. There were plantations, three fishponds cascading into each other, flower beds, and a summer house. At the far end of the third pond was a Chinese bridge. The summer house, or Fishpond Cottage, had a pointed thatched roof with Gothic diamond shaped leaded windows. Inside it was hexagon shaped with a fireplace and cupboards in two corners containing a set of china. The furniture was a green painted round table and arm chairs. In the summer Leighton would walk out from Market Weighton to the summer house where he would read the classics with the local curate.[19] This idyllic garden at the Groves is no longer.

Lookout tower, Cottingham Castle. (A. R. B. Robinson)

At Beverley, described by Edwin Waugh in 1868 as a 'garden-girdled town', the landscaped grounds of the town-houses of the gentry and the homes of the attorneys, doctors and wealthy tradesmen gave the town its 'sylvan aspect' which it fortunately retains.[20] William White looking down on the town from the Minster towers in 1858 observed the 'green spaces among the bright red roofs ...the trim flower-beds, and leafy arbours, and pebbled paths, and angular plots' which were charted in detail on the Ordnance Survey 1/1,056 map surveyed in 1853.[21] The most extensive grounds were those at Lairgate Hall, St. Mary's Manor, and Norwood House. These three were landscaped with perimeter plantations around lawns dotted with clumps and individual trees. Norwood House had a large pond with island and boat house and Lairgate Hall an extensive walled garden. Most of the other large gardens in the town, particularly those at Newbegin House and The Elms, North Bar Within are shown as principally comprising elaborate flower beds in Loudon's 'Gardenesque' style which he thought more fitting for the villa garden. The Regency period saw the contents of the garden begin to have more importance than its overall design and landscape gardening gave way to horticulture.

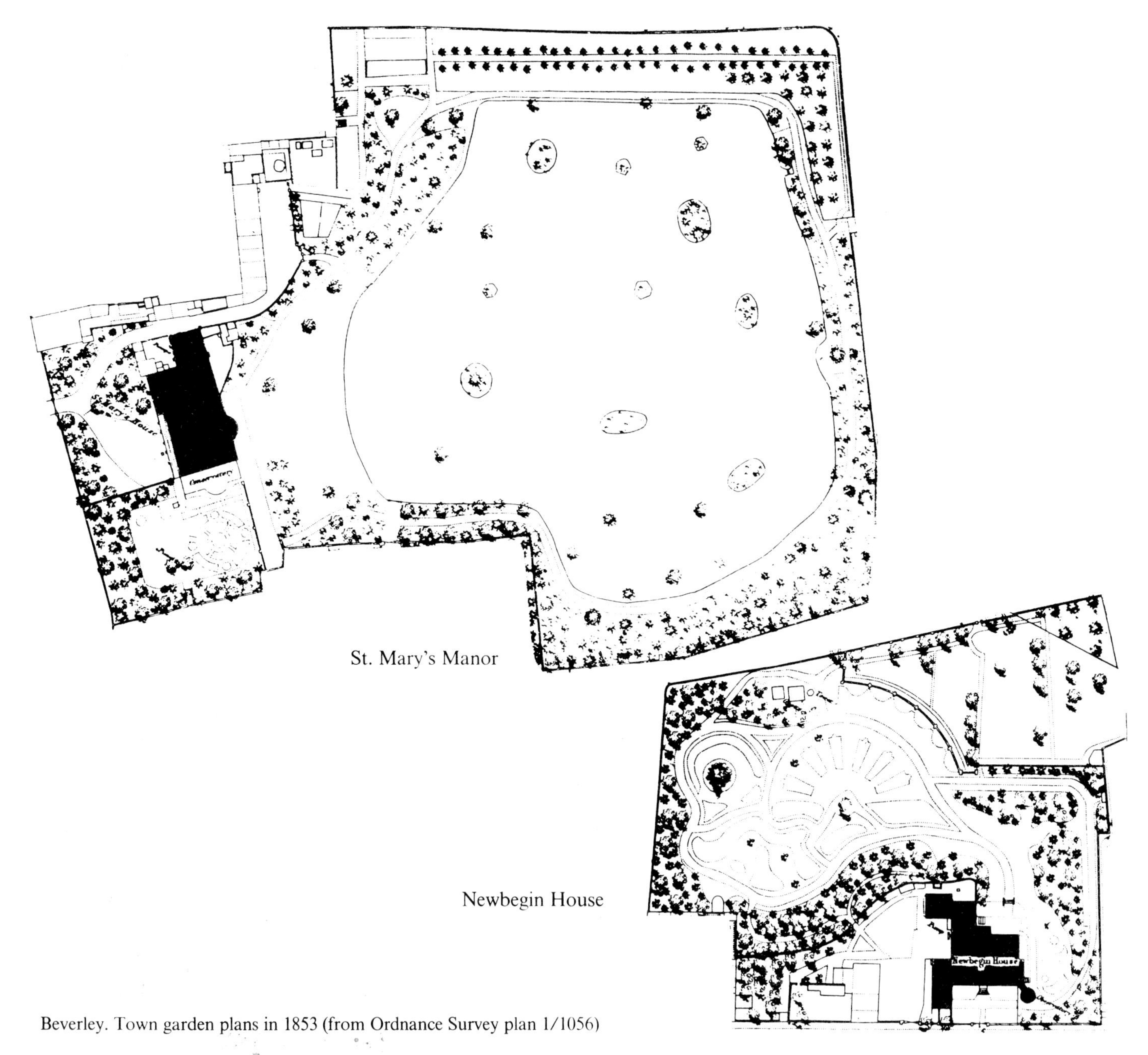

Beverley. Town garden plans in 1853 (from Ordnance Survey plan 1/1056)

Flowers had not been totally banished from the grounds of East Riding country houses in the eighteenth century but they were often confined to the walled gardens and the occasional bed near the house. It was a native of Hull the Revd. William Mason (1725-97), poet, painter, musician and landscape gardener who gave the flower garden a more prominent role in the landscape of the country house. As a garden poet Mason cannot compete with Andrew Marvell (1621-78) who was born at Winestead. Both had fathers on the staff of Holy Trinity Church, Hull, and both were pupils at Hull Grammar School. Marvell's poem *The Garden* and others on a similar theme are thought to have been written when he was staying at Nun Appleton Hall, West Riding, in 1650-52. Mason expounded his theories on landscape gardening in his long didactic poem *The English Garden* which was published in four books between 1772 and 1781. He sought to bring 'a Poet's feeling and Painter's eye' to gardening and his main innovation was the planting of irregular flower beds randomly as if the work of Nature rather than Art. This he did on a small scale at his rectory garden at Aston near Sheffield and on a grander scale at Nuneham Courtenay in Oxfordshire for Lord Harcourt 1772-79.[22]

Burton Constable, Coadstone pineapple on Orangery (Berna Moody)

The correspondence of the gardener botanist Thomas Knowlton demonstrates the great interest in new flowers and flowering shrubs, as well as more exotic plants, in the mid-eighteenth century. His letters mention acacias, asters, mesembryanthemums, passion flowers, tulips, jasmin, magnolia and periwinkle trees growing at Londesbrough. He also successfully cultivated coffee and cotton trees, guavas, melons, pawpaws, plantain, pomegranates, orange and lemon trees, sugar cane and above all pineapples.

Exotic animals as well as plants were imported into country house gardens in the eighteenth century. Deer, the principal reason for a park in the middle ages, continued to be a feature in the older parks at Burton Constable, Everingham, Londesborough, Risby, Rise and were introduced at Escrick, Scampston and Sledmere.[23] In addition menageries housing a variety of animals and birds were built at Burton Constable, Escrick and Scampston in the 1750s-60s. The menagery at Burton Constable which partially survives was designed for William Constable by Thomas Knowlton in 1760. Two years earlier Knowlton had built a greenhouse, long stoves, and fire walls to enable Constable to cultivate his exotic plants. Many of these plants are preserved in the remarkable ten volume herbarium at Burton Constable.[24]

Although Constable, Knowlton and other gentry and gardeners sought new varieties of plants from each other, or directly from abroad, their major suppliers were the increasing number of commercial nurserymen.[25] A range of London and Scottish nurseries were used by East

Riding gentry for the rarer plants but generally they dealt with Perfects of Pontefract, Telfords of York, or one of the firms in Beverley, Cottingham or Hull. At Beverley three generations of the Sigston family were nurserymen and seedsmen from the early 1730s and in 1829 the biggest employer in the town was the firm of George and Willian Tindall established 1811. Tindall's employed 50 people on their 130 acres of nurseries before they went bankrupt in 1830.[26]

A PARTNER WANTED

IN the Nurſery and Seed Buſineſs, at Beverley, Yorkſhire, a Place well ſituated for the Conveyance of Goods to almoſt all Parts of England, particularly on the Eaſtern Coaſt from Hull. It is an eſtabliſhed Nurſery, and well ſtock'd with young Stuff. Whoever may be inclinable to apply, Letters directed to Samuel Sigſton, Nurſery and Seedſman, Beverley, will be duly anſwered.

☞ Any Gentleman may be furniſhed with Fifty Thouſand Italian or Lombardy Poplars, from 6 to 10 Feet high, at 18 s. per Hundred.—Two Hundred Thouſand tranſplanted Scotch Firs, 18 Inches and 2 Feet high, at 50 s. per Thouſand.—Three Years old Beech, well rooted and good Plants, 2 and 3 Feet high, at 40 s. per Thouſand.

At the ſame Place may be had, Foreſt-Trees, Fruit-Trees, and Flowering Shrubs; alſo Garden, Graſs, and Flower Seeds.

York Courant 5 December 1775

Part of the catalogue of Stephen Garraway, a London seedsman, sent to John Grimston of Kilnwick *c.* 1770 (Humberside County Archive Office)

A CATALOGUE of Garden, Graſs, Tree, and Flower Seeds, Flower Roots, Plants, Nets, &c. Sold by STEPHEN GARRAWAY, Seedſman and Net-Maker, at the ROSE, near the *Globe* Tavern, *Fleetſtreet*, LONDON.

GARDEN PEAS.

Golden, Charlton, Ormorit's, Reading or Long, Maſter's or Short } Hotſpur
Early, Leadman's, Crooked Sugar } Dwarf
Marrowfat
Blue Union
Spaniſh Moretta
Nonpareil
Rouncival
Crown or Roſe

GARDEN BEANS.

Early Barbary or Mazagan

White, Green curl'd, Broad leav'd } Endive
Upright, Solid } Celery
Dwarf Celeriack
Great rooted, Curl'd, Common } Parſley
Red, White } Beet
Round leav'd, Prickly, French } Spinach
Sorrel
Cauliflower
White, Purple } Brocoli
Early Yorkſhire

Yellow Jaccea
Canterbury Bells
* Flos Adonis
* Devil in a Buſh
* Chriſanthemum
* Xeranthemum
* Tobacco
* Buſh Bazil
* Love lies Bleeding
* Princes Feather
Primroſe Tree
* Love Apple
Thorn Apple
* Cyenus, or Bottles
* Major, * Minor } Convolvulus, Blue and Scarlet
* Globe Thiſtle
* Double China Aſter
* Hawk's Eye

Fenochia
Nettle
Carraway
Cummin
Annis
Coriander
Gromil
Henbane
Plantane
Fenugreek
Burdock
Peony
Daucus
Oculus Chriſti
Linn or Flax
Brown Muſtard
Broom
Gourd
Pumpkin

BULBOUS *and* FIBEROUS ROOTED FLOWERS.

Red, White and Blue, Double and Single Hyacinths
Turkey and Scarlet Ranuncula
Double Enemonies, in Sorts
Tulips
Iris, all Sorts
Narciſſus
Double Jonquils
Crocus
Crown Imperial
Lillies
Martagon
Guernſey Lilly
Italian Tuberoſe
Frittilaria
Fraxanella

The kitchen garden and the estate gardener are neglected themes in the history of gardening. Credit is often given to a landowner when it should really go to his head gardener. In many cases the gardener is little more than a name in estate accounts but some gained prominence through other activities or publications. The importance of Thomas Knowlton has already been mentioned. One of his predecessors at Londesborough was Roger Looker, who in 1681, along with George London, superintendent of the Royal Gardens after 1688, was a founder of the Brompton Park Nursery, which Evelyn said 'was the greatest work of the kind ever seen, or heard of, either in Books or Travels'.[27] The Victoria and Albert Museum now stands on the site of this nursery. In the 1750s-60s Thomas Kyle, later the author of a work on the management of peaches and nectarines, was gardener at Burton Constable, and William Speechley (1734-1819) who afterwards published books on the cultivation of the pineapple and the vine was gardener at Scampston. Speechley is said to have perhaps 'surpassed every practical Gardener of his age'.[28] William Pontey (d.1831) a leading arboriculturist and author of *The Profitable Planter,* 1800, *The Forest Pruner, or Timber owners assistant*, 1805, and *The Rural Improver*, 1823, was head gardener at Kilnwick for some years.

Gardeners, nurserymen and interested gentry and tradesmen met together in florists' societies. At York the 'Royal Society of Gardiners and Lovers of a Garden, within the City and County of York' was holding annual 'feasts' or shows from the early 18th century, and in 1768 the still flourishing Ancient Society of York Florists was formed.[29] Florists were regularly meeting at Malton by 1748.[30] No such early society has been recorded at Hull but there were enthusiastic botanists amongst the tradesmen and professionals. Dr. William Chambers (d.1785) was described as 'a grate lover and observer of plants and nature'[31], and two members of Hull merchant families Peter William Watson (1761-1830) and Adrian Hardy Haworth (1768-1833) gained more than local fame for their botanical writings. Watson, who lived at Tudor House, Thwaite Street, Cottingham 1806-30 was the author of *Dendrologia Britannica*, 1824-5, a beautifully illustrated book in two volumes dealing with exotic shrubs and trees growing in English parks and woods. Haworth was the leading authority on succulent plants during the first part of the nineteenth century and the author of many books and papers about them. He lived at Hallgate House, Hallgate, Cottingham and was the brother of Benjamin Blaydes Haworth (1763-1836) of Haworth Hall and a friend of John Claudius Loudon (1783-1843). Haworth assisted Richard Steele with his work *An Essay upon Gardening*, published at York in 1793, for which many East Yorkshire gentry subscribed.[32]

Watson and Haworth were two of the founders of the Hull Botanic Garden established in 1812 on a six-acre site at the end of the aptly named Linnaeus Street. This botanic garden, which illustrated the enthusiasm for plants and gardening in the town, was one of the first to be established in a provincial town and marked the beginning of the change in emphasis in horticulture and landscaping from landscaped park to public park, a change that culminated in the great municipal parks of late Victorian England. In the late twentieth century, through the work of the National Trust and private owners in restoring and revitalising their gardens, the emphasis and interest has returned to the grounds of the country house.

Hull Botanic Garden from *Greenwood's Picture of Hull*, 1835.

REFERENCES

1. quoted in D. Woodward, *Descriptions of East Yorkshire: Leland to Defoe*, East Yorkshire Local History Society, 1985, pp.50-51
2. M. Wilson, *William Kent Architect, Designer, Painter, Gardener*, London, 1984
3. H. Walpole, *Anecdotes of Painting in England*, vol.3, London, 1888, pp.81-82 from his essay 'On Modern Gardening' written 1770
4. D. Jacques, *Georgian Gardens*, London, 1983, p.34
5. A. Pope, *Epistles to Several Persons*, ed. F. W. Bateson, London, 1951, p.137
6. B. Henrey, *No Ordinary Gardener : Thomas Knowlton 1691 – 1781*, London, 1986, p.15
7. Jacques, *Georgian Gardens*, pp.40-41
8. Yorkshire Archaeological Society MS 328
9. *York Courant* 24/9/1754, 23/12/1755
10. D. Stroud, *Capability Brown*, Faber and Faber, London, 1975
11. D. Turnbull, 'Thomas White (1739-1811): Eighteenth century Landscape Designer and Arboriculturist', unpublished Ph.D thesis, University of Hull, 1990; D. Neave, 'The Search for Thomas White', *Georgian Society for East Yorkshire Newsletter*, 11, 1984
12. Hull University Library (HUL) DDJL/3/1
13. 'Wassand Hall'. *Georgian Society for East Yorkshire Trasactions*, vol.5, pt.1, 1958-61, p.34
14. J. J. Sheahan and T. Whellan, *History and Topography of York and the East Riding*, vol.2, Beverley, 1856, pp.384-5
15. quoted in J. Crowther, *Descriptions of East Yorkshire De La Pryme to Head*, East Yorkshire Local History Society, 1992, pp.32-33
16. A. Young, *A Six Months' Tour through the North of England*, London, 1770, vol.1, p.169; Humberside County Archive Office (HCAO) Accession 1045, plan
17. A. R. B. Robinson, *The Counting House*, York, 1992, pp.94-6
18. M. T. Craven, *A History of the Borough of Hedon*, Hull, 1972, pp.46-7
19. 'History of Goodmanham', typescript, *c*.1930
20. P. Brown, *Old Beverley*, East Yorkshire Local History Society, 1983, pp.[2-3]
21. W. White, *A Month in Yorkshire*, London, 1858, p.48
22. M. Batey, 'William Mason, English Gardener', *Garden History*, vol.1, no.2, Feb. 1973, pp.11-25; see also B. Barr and J. Ingamells, *A Candidate for Praise: William Mason 1725-97 Precentor of York*, York Festival, 1973
23. Susan Neave, *Medieval Parks of East Yorkshire*, Hutton Press, 1991
24. E. Hall 'The plant collections of an eighteenth-century virtuoso', *Garden History*, vol.14, no.1, Spring 1986, pp.6-26; I and E Hall, *Burton Constable Hall*, Hull City Museums and Art Galleries and Hutton Press, 1991, pp.33-40
25. J. Harvey, *Early Nurserymen*, Chichester, 1974
26. K. J. Allison (ed.), *Victoria County History, East Riding*, vol.6, Oxford, 1989, p.117
27. quoted in G. W. Johnson, *A History of English Gardening*, London, 1829, p.116
28. ibid., p.239
29. R. Duthie, *Florists' Flowers and Societies*, Princes Risborough, 1988, pp.14-5, 19, 21
30. *York Courant*, 2/8/1748
31. B. Henrey, *No Ordinary Gardener*, pp.89-99; There was a Society of Florists in Hull by 1824, *Hull Advertiser* 13/2/1824
32. A. H. Haworth, *Complete Works on Succulent Plants*, London, 1965, vol.1, pp.9-57 Introduction by W. T. Stearn.

GAZETTEER

BIRDSALL

Birdsall House, 5 miles south-east of Malton, has one of the finest landscape settings of any East Yorkshire country house. Built initially around 1600 for the Sotheby family the house was altered and extended by the Willoughby family in the eighteenth and nineteenth centuries. Thomas Willoughby (1694-1742) who had married the heiress Elizabeth Sotheby in 1719 began the creation of the present landscape. He was the younger son of the first Lord Middleton, and grandson of the 17th century naturalist Francis Willoughby, and succeeded to Birdsall on the death of Thomas Sotheby in November 1729.

Thomas Willoughby seems to have already been running the estate before his father-in-law's death for in October 1729 he asked Thomas Knowlton, the gardener from Londesborough, to visit Birdsall presumably to advise on the gardens. It is not clear if Knowlton visited Birdsall on this occasion but in mid November 1729 he was 'at a gentleman's seat ... for two or three days on account of measuring his ground for a new design for a garden and paddock and shall be that way again within a month'. It is very likely that Knowlton drew up the plan of Birdsall dated 1730. The plan shows a layout with similarities to the contemporary Rococo gardens at Londesborough and South Dalton, with which Knowlton was associated, but without any of their meandering walks. A straight walk cut through the plantation in Gisderdale to the south west of the house opens out into a circular clearing before ending at a sharp point. The series of ponds created in the valley directly west of the house are also given geometric shapes and further west circular clumps of trees are shown in fields adjoining the garden. Willoughby seemingly had an interest in gardening for his name appears in the list of subscribers to Philip Miller's *Gardeners Dictionary*, 1731 and he sought Knowlton's assistance on at least one other occasion in 1736.

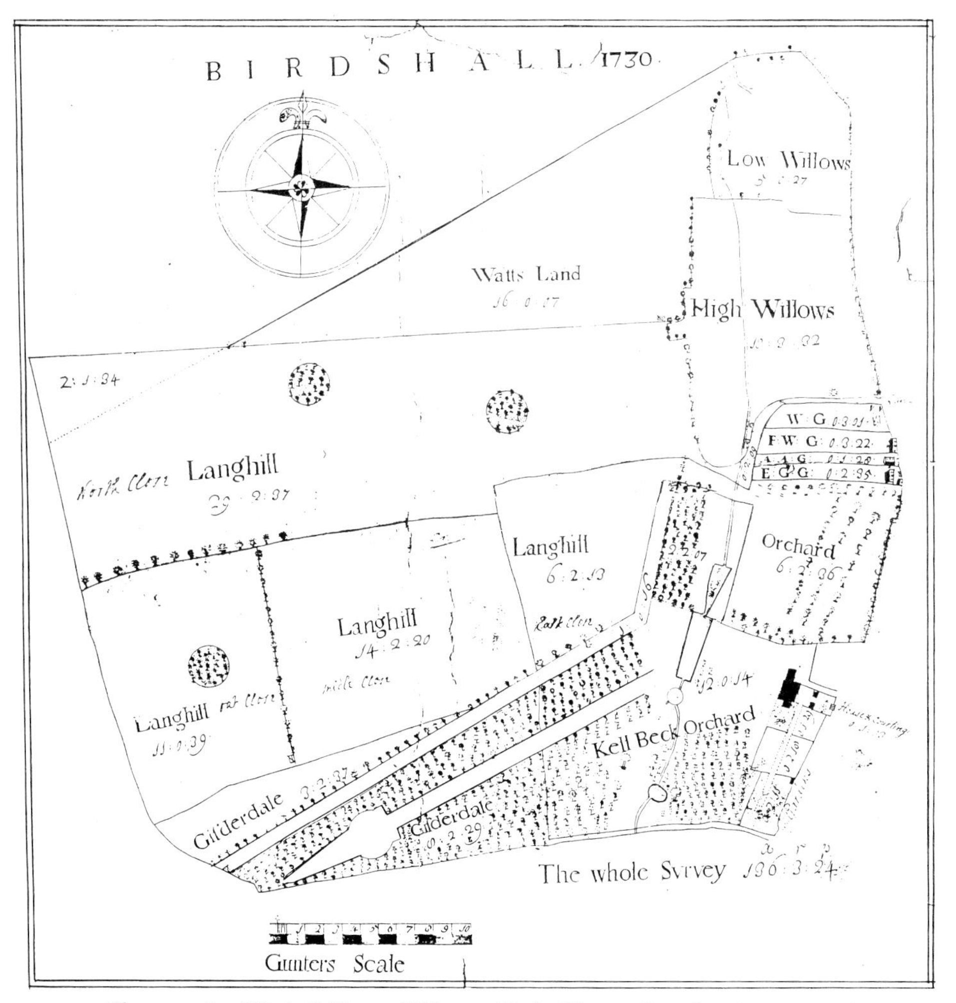

The grounds of Birdsall House, 1730, possibly by Thomas Knowlton (Lord Middleton)

A second undated plan possibly of *c.*1760, records a number of changes which had given the landscape a more natural appearance. The long walk had become a simple track through enlarged and less regular plantations, the fields to the west had lost their hedges, and the ground to the east of the house had been

Birdsall House from the North-west across the bottom lake. (Hull University Photograhic Service)

laid out as parkland. This extension of the park had been made possible by a diversion of the old village road away from the house and church. North of the house a kitchen garden had been built. Within the grounds a third much larger pond or lake had been added, the cascades between the ponds emphasised and above the circular basin an almost circular open area is shown. This last is said to have been prepared as a platform for the temple which the architect Sir William Chambers designed for Henry Willoughby (d.1800). Although never built the temple is illustrated in Chamber's *Treatise on Civil Architecture* published in 1759.

Henry Willoughby, who succeeded as 5th Lord Middleton in 1781, may have employed the landscape gardener Thomas White. White's bank account records payments totalling £128 from a [Mr.] Willoughby in 1776-7. These may relate to the further enlargement of the park westwards and the extensive planting around the grounds which are shown on Bryant's 1829 map of the East Riding. By this date the ruined church had become a picturesque feature of the landscape near the house. This followed the building of a new church on the edge of the park in 1823-4.

Birdsall House is the home of Lord and Lady Middleton and the grounds are private.

[Plans at Birdsall; B. Henrey, *No ordinary gardener: Thomas Knowlton 1691-1781*, British Museum (Natural History), 1986]

See colour plate p.40

Design for temple for Henry Willoughby of Birdsall by Sir William Chambers (from W. Chambers, Treatise on Civil Architecture, *1759)*

Birdsall House from the east showing ruined church on the right (Hull University Photographic Service)

BOYNTON

The splendid mid-eighteenth century painting by Arthur Devis, in the Ferens Art Gallery, Hull which depicts Sir George and Lady Strickland in parkland by a serpentine river or lake in a hilly landscape unfortunately does not appear to be a portrayal of the grounds of their home, Boynton Hall, two miles west of Bridlington.

Sir George's father, Sir William Strickland (d.1735) who extensively remodelled the late 16th century hall with the advice of Lord Burlington was also active in improving its landscape. Around 1725 he obtained about a hundred larch trees from Switzerland which were planted out in small detached clumps. This was a pioneering use of larch and these trees were reputed to be 'the parent-stock of most of the larch-trees in the North of England',[1]

More extensive plantations were made by Sir George Strickland, of whom it was said in 1757 that he 'minds nothing but planting children and trees'. The parkland around the house was greatly enlarged. In 1768 he had the main Bridlington road diverted to the north and the public road running south to Carnaby closed off at the church. A walk was laid out through the large plantation to the south of the house which led up across Wold Gate, an ancient routeway, to the octagonal tower known as Carnaby Temple. The Temple, placed on the crest of the hill by Sir George around 1770, provided extensive views over Bridlington Bay. A more circuitous route back to the hall from the Temple led through Hallow Kiln Wood and under the Fond Bridge which carries the Wold Gate across the valley. This 18th century ornamental bridge is built of brick with rough-hewn stone dressings.

Boynton Hall, Gothick garden house (Hull University Photographic Service)

Nearer the hall are a number of ornamental buildings in the grounds. In the south-west corner of the gardens is the charming Gothick garden house. This late 16th century brick building was Gothicised around 1770. The east end of the greenhouse was similarly ornamented with round-arched arcades, and Lady Strickland's dairy, south of the hall, was given Gothick details.

To the north of the hall the Gipsey Race was widened to form a long narrow serpentine lake. To the south east in Fishponds Wood an irregular series of lakes in the picturesque manner were created, possibly in the early nineteenth century.

In 1793 the author and poet Anna Seward when staying at Bridlington Quay went to visit 'a sweet sequestered umbrageous glen, where Lady Strickland has erected a farm-house and a dairy-house in the Dutch style, a brook intersects the circular meadow, and flows around the buildings, resembling the dikes of Holland, with Dutch bridges over it.'[2] This was seemingly not at Boynton but was the 'agreeable retreat called the Dutch farm ... furnished in the Dutch style with articles from Holland ... used as an occasional tea room by the Strickland family' which in 1830 stood a little distance to the south of Carnaby village.[3] The site of this East Yorkshire version of Marie Antoinette's hamlet at the Petit Trianon is at Carnaby station where there is a moated area enclosing irregular ponds cut through by the Hull-Bridlington railway line.

The grounds at Boynton Hall, the home of Mr. and Mrs. Richard Marriott, are private although there are public footpaths along the periphery.

Carnaby Temple

1. H. E. Strickland, *A General View of the Agriculture of the East Riding of Yorkshire*, 1812, pp.186-7
2. J. Crowther (ed.), *Descriptions of East Yorkshire: De La Pryme to Head*. East Yorkshire Local History Society, 1992, p.33
3. *Picturesque Excursions from Bridlington Quay being a Descriptive Guide to the most interesting scenery in that neighbourhood*, Bridlington, 1830, p.18

See colour plate p.41

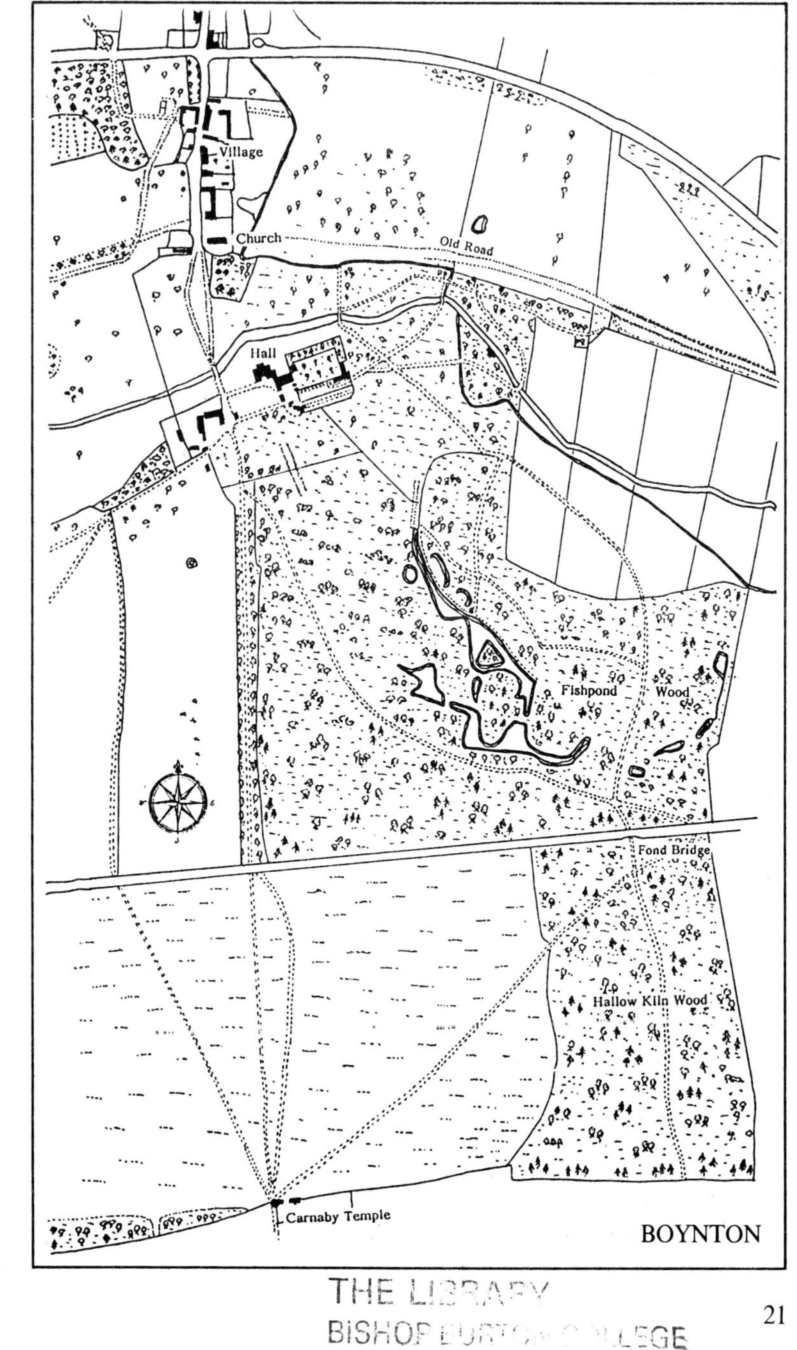

Boynton Hall grounds *c.*1850 based on the 1st edition O.S. 6″ plan

BURTON CONSTABLE

Situated 7 miles to the north-east of Hull, on the flat Holderness plain, 66 feet above sea level, Burton Constable became the principal seat of the Constable family in the late sixteenth century. An anonymous painting of Burton Constable Hall in the late seventeenth century shows the house fronted by a plain, walled, formal garden with an area of parkland stretching behind to the west. This parkland where deer were kept from the sixteenth to the late nineteenth centuries is shown as a large circular area enclosed by a pale on Warburton's map of Yorkshire of 1720. The same map shows an avenue of trees stretching southwards from the house. Other plans show that there were also avenues leading east, west and south west and a line of fishponds in the park. From the future site of the kitchen gardens an avenue led north to the ancient North Wood.

William Constable (1721-91) inherited the family estate in 1747 and in the mid-1750s set about modernising the Elizabethan house and improving the surrounding parkland which he described as a 'wilderness' with swamps, 'gorse and whin higher than a man on horseback'. With the assistance of the gardener Thomas Knowlton from Londesborough, the architect Timothy Lightoler, and the landscape designers Thomas White and Capability Brown, Constable created a thriving and productive garden and a splendid landscape park. Exotic and ornamental plants were collected and cultivated in a kitchen garden with a hot house designed by Lightoler with Knowlton's advice. During the years 1758-68 the kitchen garden was under the management of a most able Scottish gardener Thomas Kyle who was later the author of *A treatise on the management of peaches and nectarines* (1783). In addition Constable formed a fine collection of botanical specimens recorded in a ten volume herbarium.

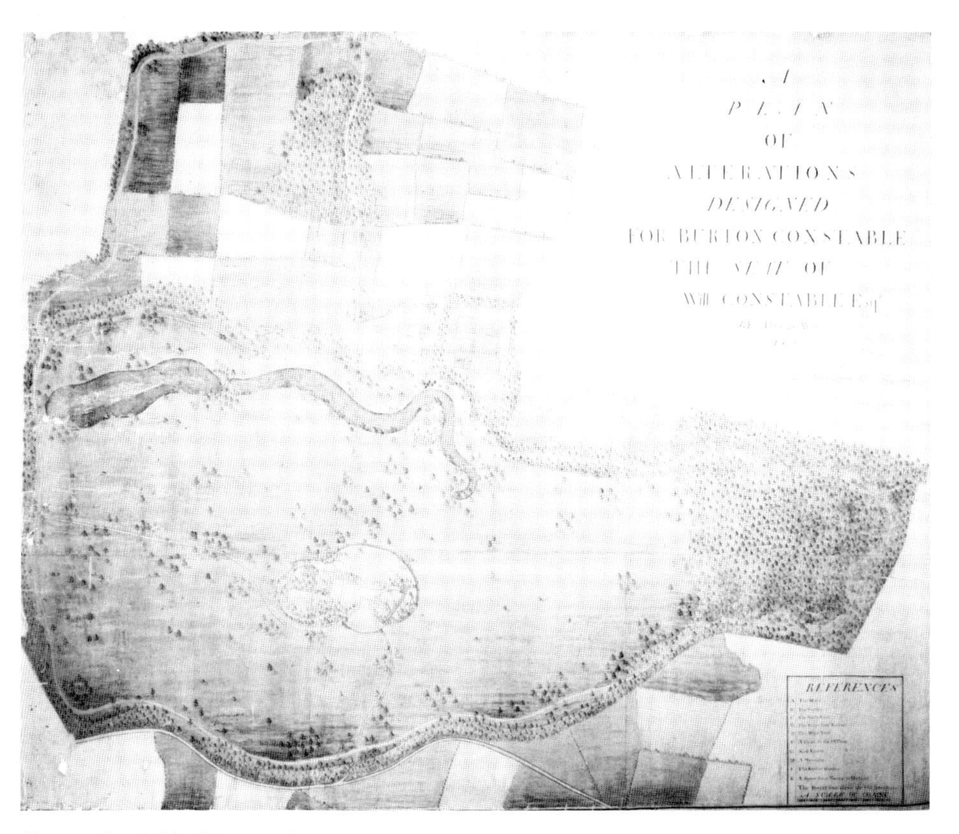

Burton Constable. Plan for alterations by Thomas White, 1768 (Burton Constable – Leeds City Art gallery)

William Constable undertook three Grand Tours to the continent between 1741 and 1771 and returned from each with new ideas and contacts to aid in the transformation of his property. To design a landscape garden he called upon the services of Capability Brown in 1767. Brown's initial proposal was rejected but he produced several further plans and drawings for the estate and visited Constable at least nine times between 1769 and 1782. Designs were also obtained from Timothy Lightoler and from Thomas White. White, who had been employed elsewhere as foreman to Brown until 1765, drew up a large and colourful watercolour design in 1768, for which he charged 10 guineas. This plan eliminated entirely the formal garden, the straight tree lined avenues to the west and south of the house, and introduced instead clumped and specimen trees on the lawns with shelter belts of trees

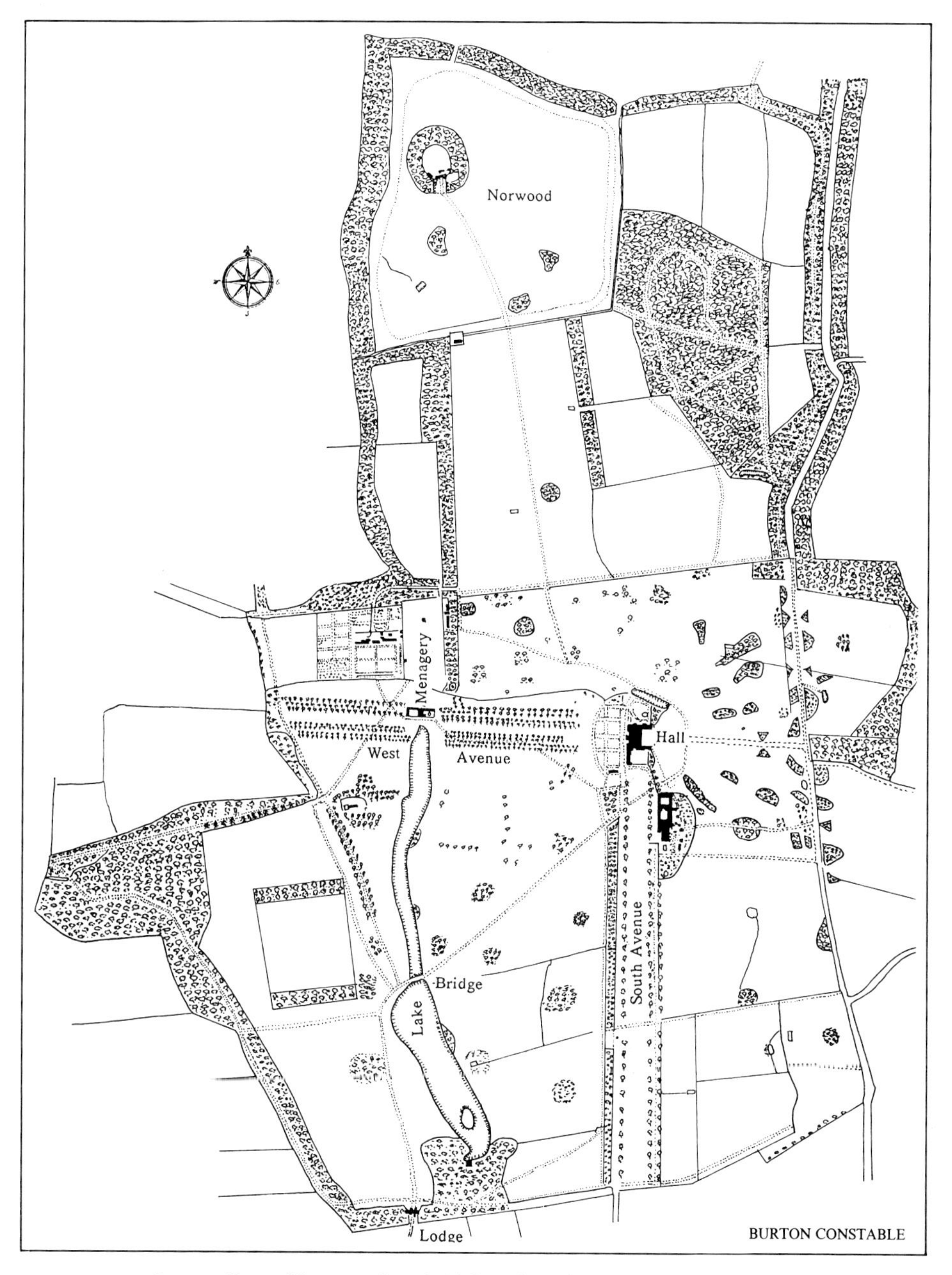

Burton Constable grounds, c.1850 based on the 1st edition O.S. 6" plan

around the periphery of the park.

White's plan was not implemented and from 1772 William Constable and Capability Brown worked closely together to execute the latter's designs. Brown may have incorporated some of White's suggestions into his own proposals. Trees were planted to the north and south of the house and a ha-ha encircled the lawn following the line of the old moat. On the east side of the house the avenue was removed and clumps of trees planted. Where White had suggested disposing of the straight avenues of trees to the south and west, Brown decided to retain them and not disturb the mature native elm and chestnut trees. Large quantities of elms, limes, planes, birch, beech, alders, larch, and yew were acquired from various nurseries and planted in the late 1770s. Work on creating the lake, divided by a dam cleverly disguised by Brown's brick and stone bridge, was begun in 1775. A new entranceway to Sproatley was created, framed by a Gothic style castellated gateway designed by James Wyatt in 1785.

George Barrett's painting of 1777 (see p.44), shows the east front of the house, looking out upon a peaceful park setting, with the towers designed by Capability Brown for the south courtyard appearing over the shrubbery to the left. Although Brown proposed placing other architectural features in the landscape, his ideas were not adopted and in the nineteenth century Sir Clifford Constable erected a large stone pedestal surmounted by a stag on Roe Hill where Brown had proposed a temple or arch. Within the gardens there was built the fine neo-classical, seven-bayed orangery, topped with Coade-stone urns, pineapples and statues designed in 1788 by Thomas

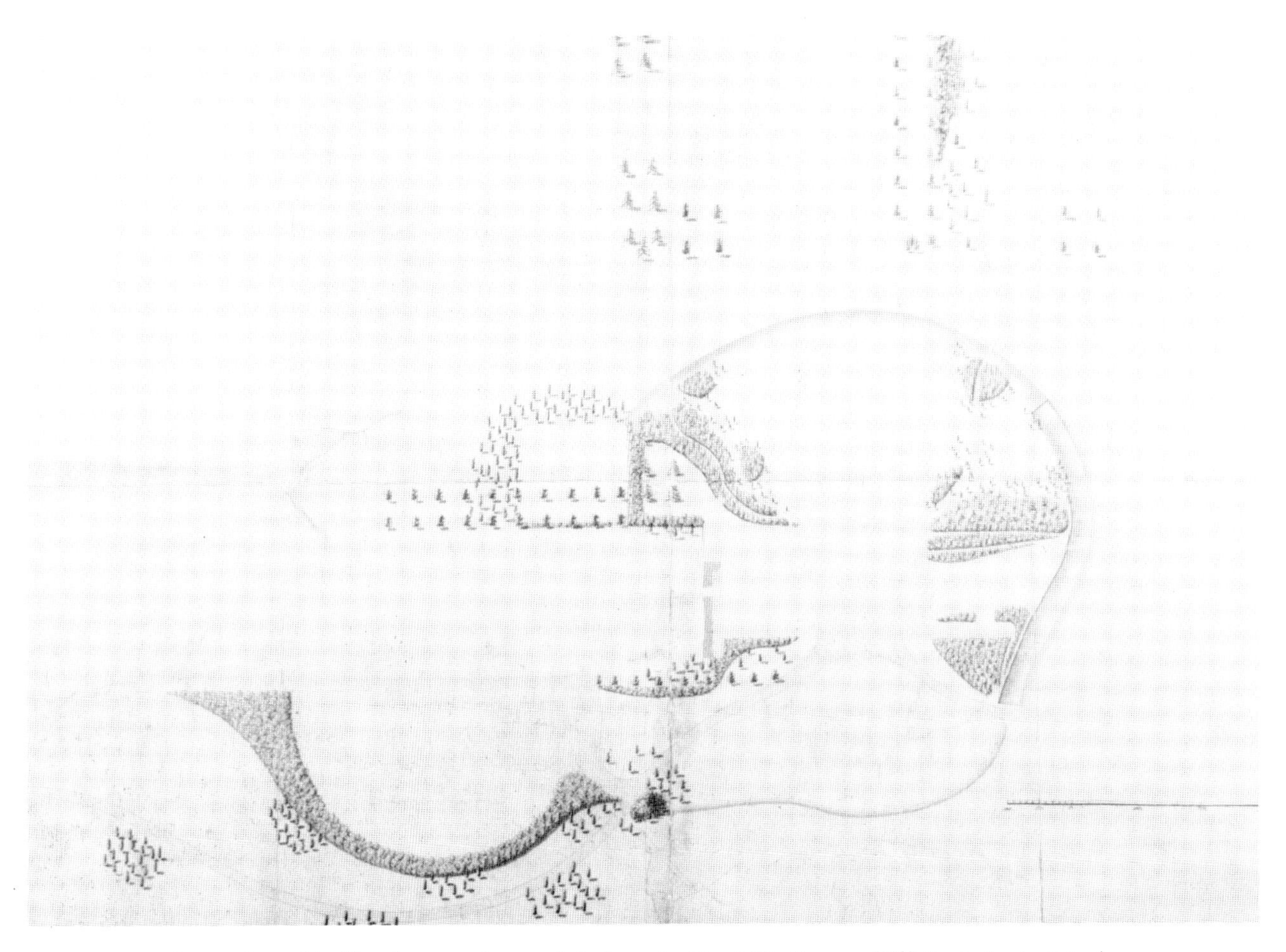

Burton Constable. Plan for grounds around the house by Capability Brown **c.**1769 (Leeds City Art Gallery)

Atkinson of York. This has been recently restored.

The nineteenth century saw alterations to the grounds, including the reinstatement of the south and west avenues which had been thinned rather than removed by Brown. The 100 acre North Wood was cut down in the 1790s and later a private racecourse with grandstand was built on its site. The reversion to formality prevalent in the Victorian era occurred near the house with the creation of a French Garden containing walks lined with yews and copies of antique statues, now sadly in a poor state owing to the disintegration of the artificial stone.

[This entry is based mainly on the writings and research of Elisabeth Hall in particular 'The plant collections of an eighteenth-century virtuoso', *Garden History*, vol.14, no.1, Spring 1986, pp.6-26 and 'Constable the improver — the creation of a landscape garden' in I. and E. Hall, *Burton Constable Hall*, Hull City Museums and Art Galleries and Hutton Press, 1991, pp.68-70. In these articles much more is said on Brown's layout and the plants used in the park and gardens.]

See colour plates p.44 and back cover.

Burton Constable. The menagery designed by Thomas Knowlton, c.1762

Burton Constable. The orangery designed by Thomas Atkinson, 1788

CAVE CASTLE, SOUTH CAVE

In 1783 Henry Boldero Barnard succeeded to the Manor of South Cave East Hall and he soon set about rebuilding the modest house and improving its setting. Firstly he vigorously promoted the enclosure of the extensive open fields which was accomplished in 1785-7. This gave him a substantial block of land to the north and east of his house. In the area to the south of East Hall Barnard exchanged lands with the vicar, removed the vicarage house to the Market Place, realigned the road further south and closed a public footpath across his grounds. In 1787 he commissioned the landscape gardener William Emes to draw up plans for improving the enlarged grounds. No improvement plan is known to exist but some idea of the changes made can be gleaned by comparing the fine plan of South Cave produced by Edward Geldart in 1759 with the first edition 6″ Ordnance Survey plan of 1855.

The 1759 plan suggests that there were modest formal gardens around East Hall. Avenues are shown running north and south from the house, the latter towards a rectangular 'canal' which was across the road in Bull Pasture. In 1787 the road was re-sited to the south of the 'canal' in a hollow out of sight of the house allowing uninterrupted views across to a new area of parkland created from the Bull Pasture and adjoining fields towards the Humber. The canal was enlarged and transformed into an irregular lake with a small island. The park was extended northwards with an arm going eastward to the Weighton Road where a castellated entrance lodge was built. The parkland was surrounded by a narrow band of plantations and to the north of the house the Wilderness was created with winding paths, a summer

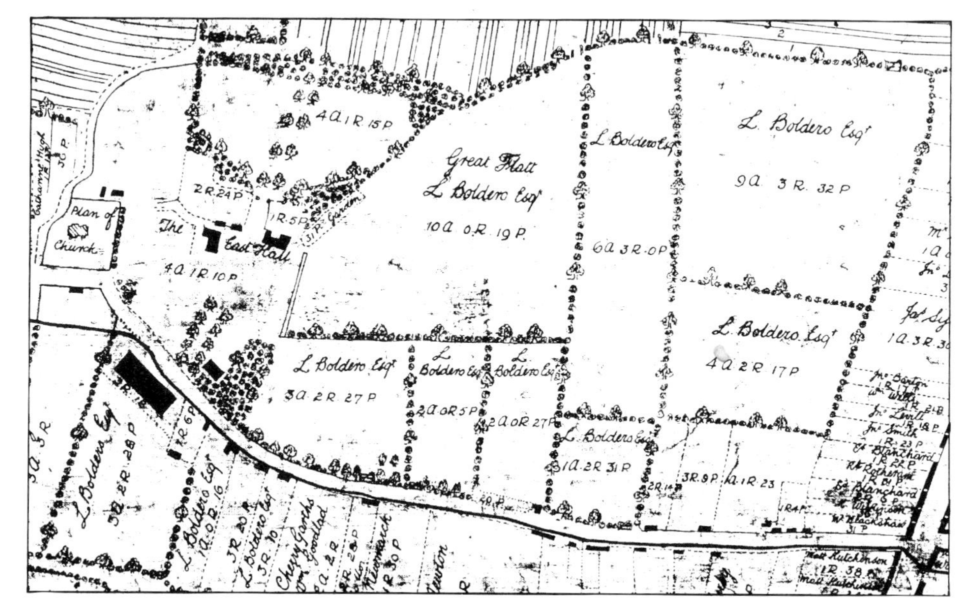

The grounds of East Hall, South Cave, from Edward Geldart's plan of 1759. (reproduced by permission of Hull University Archivist, Brynmor Jones library)

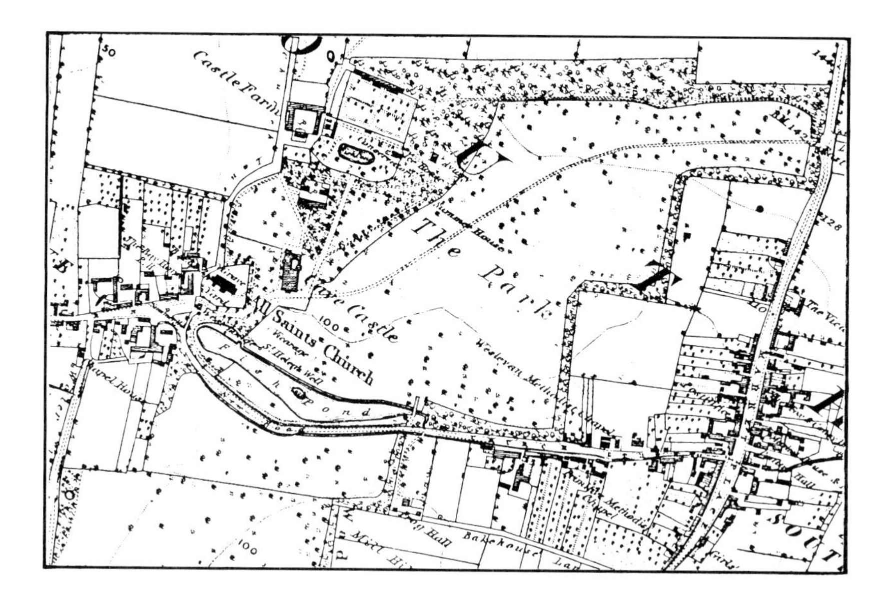

Cave Castle grounds, 1855, from first edition O.S. 6″ plan

South Cave, Cave Castle, 1812 (*from J. Bigland,* The Beauties of England and Wales, *1812*)

house an ice house and aviary. Here also was placed the kitchen garden and by the mid nineteenth century a pond, lawn and large conservatory.

The setting improved Barnard then rebuilt East Hall in castellated Gothick and renamed the house Cave Castle c.1791. Although the Castle is now a hotel and much of the parkland has been built upon many of the eighteenth century landscape features remain.

[see David Neave (ed.) *South Cave: A market village community in the 18th and 19th centuries*, Mr. Pye Books, Howden, 1984; R. A. Alec-Smith 'Cave Castle', *The Georgian Society for East Yorkshire Transactions*, Vol.IV, pt.III, 1956-8, pp.50-60.]

ESCRICK

In the mid nineteenth century the 450 acre park surrounding Escrick Hall, six miles south of York, was one of the largest in the East Riding of Yorkshire. It was a comparatively recent creation, for until the 1780s the hall had stood in modest grounds adjoining the church and rectory in the centre of a sizeable village surrounded by open arable fields. The hall built c.1680 by Henry Thompson, the son of a successful York wine merchant, was refronted in 1758 and further altered and enlarged to the designs of John Carr in 1763-5.

Carr had also drawn up a general plan of the whole ground about the house and laid out a way across the open fields to the 'menagerie' a mile to the south in 1763. This avenue which still can be seen is shown on Jeffery's plan of 1772. Menagerie Farm remains but nothing is known of when, or what, wild animals were kept there. It had probably been built by Beilby Thompson, who inherited the estate in 1750. He was presumably the 'Esqr Thompson' whom the Londesborough gardener Thomas Knowlton reported in February 1758 as having 'a plantain tree' in fruit

> *in excellent order but then he has a fine stove 25 feet high all crown glass in front & slope that in summer it draws with an equality of the hottest climate in East or West Indies so that his pines are beyond any body else.*

Escrick Park from the south by N. Whittlock. (T. Allen, *History of Yorkshire*, 1831)

In 1781 Beilby Thompson proposed enclosing the open fields and he obtained an Act of Parliament to remove the old church and rectory and so improve the surroundings of the hall. Following enclosure a new church and rectory were built to the north of the village. The old church and rectory and twenty-six cottages were demolished and the roads from Selby, Stillingfleet and Howden were diverted to allow for the creation of a modest park to the south of the hall by 1809. In 1825 P.B. Thompson, Lord Wenlock moved the Howden and Selby roads further east and west respectively and the park considerably enlarged extending southwards to link up with the large area of ancient woodland known as Holly Carr and Hart Nooking. It was seemingly at this date that the Ionic Temple was built near the Menagerie and a walk laid out to it. Deer were introduced and two duck decoys created on the eastern side. Extensive planting took place in the park with some trees grouped in large clumps but no distinctive landscaping is evident. Surprisingly with the close proximity of a stream no lake was provided. Near the house, in the flower garden, there was a thatched root house.

Much of the former parkland has now returned to arable except near to the hall where ridge and furrow still indicate the position of open field strips. Queen Margaret's School occupies Escrick Hall and the grounds are private.

[see David Neave and Ivan Hall, 'Escrick Hall and Park', *York Georgian Society Annual Report*, 1971, pp.25-33; K. J. Allison, *The East Riding of Yorkshire Landscape*, 1976, pp.184-6]

EVERINGHAM

Everingham lies in the Vale of York four miles south of Pocklington. There was a deer park there in the late thirteenth century which in 1635 covered some 380 acres. The estate was owned by the Constable family and their descendants from the early sixteenth century. Although records are patchy three phases of landscaping of the grounds around the hall can be identified in the eighteenth and early nineteenth centuries.

The first phase took place in the years 1730-43 when the then owner Sir Marmaduke Constable was in self-imposed exile on the continent. Letters written to and from Dom John Bede Potts, his estate steward and chaplain, record considerable activity in planting and 'improving' in and around the park. Advice and practical assistance was provided by Thomas Knowlton, Lord Burlington's gardener at nearby Londesborough. A broad avenue was planted running south from the hall across Harswell Road to the beck in Everingham Carrs, another lesser avenue was planted going west and a green walk was laid out around two fish ponds.

The rebuilding of Everingham Hall for William Haggerston Constable to the designs of John Carr in 1757-64 inevitably led to improvements in the grounds. The common fields of Everingham were the subject of an enclosure act in 1765 but this did little more than confirm an existing situation. A new kitchen garden was built and planted and there is mention of a sunk fence in 1764-5. It is probable that it was at this date that the serpentine lake, shown on a plan of 1806, was dug and the clumps of trees and boundary plantations placed in the park. Considerable activity in the gardens is recorded in the late 1760s-70s. In April 1778 the steward reported: 'Mr James Bayne seems to go well on with his business, planting, thinning the shruberys, etc, and the kitchen garden makes a very different appearance for the better than it has done for many years past'.

The third phase of landscaping was carried out for William Constable-Maxwell (1804-76) who inherited the Everingham estate in 1819. As well as improvements to the grounds he was responsible for considerable rebuilding in the village, the building of the magnificent Roman Catholic chapel 1836-39 and major extensions to the hall 1845-48. The grounds were improved 1826-7 under the supervision of a little known landscape gardener, J. N. Sleed of Kensington, seemingly an exponent of the picturesque style of J. C. Loudon one of whose books, possibly the *Encyclopaedia of Gardening,* he sent to Constable-Maxwell.

Everingham Hall from the west
(Hull University Photographic Service)

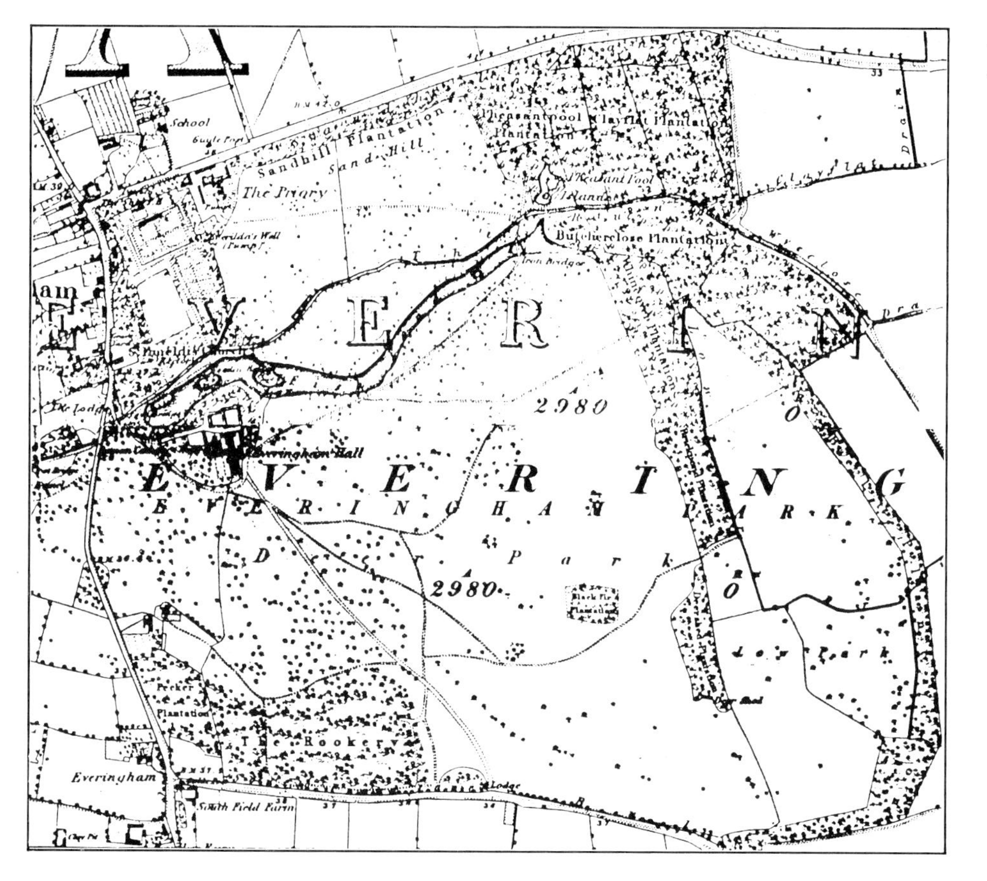

Everingham Park, 1855, from the first edition O.S. 6" plan.

Constable-Maxwell's notes in his memorandum book under 1 April 1826: 'Sleed came down to give his plans respecting any alteration he might deem fit in the Pleasure Gardens, Park, etc.'. Sleed proposed that 'the present road beyond the Drawing Room windows' to the west be removed 'fifty yards into the meadow so as to conceal it when looking from the house and to extend the Pleasure Ground on that side'. This extension of the park necessitated the removal of two cottages. A new entrance road was also planned from the Thorpe road to the north-east, it was to cross the lake by an iron bridge, and the lake itself was to be increased in size. On 3 May 1827 Constable-Maxwell recorded that he had 'opened the new village road and laid the foundation of the lodge'. But on that day he also determined 'to exchange the back road up to the house and bring it thro' the Hall Garth and form a pleasure ground'. Alterations and additions to the park continued, an ice house was built in 1828, a south lodge on the Harswell road in 1841 and in 1867 the pleasure gardens to the north of the hall were enhanced by the building of the small classical oratory.

Everingham Hall, reduced to its mid-eighteenth century size, still retains much of its eighteenth and early nineteenth century landscape, including the large lake. The grounds are private.

[HUL DDEV; B. Henrey, *No ordinary gardener: Thomas Knowlton 1691-1781*, British Museum (Natural History), 1986; P. Roebuck, *Constable of Everingham Estate Correspondence 1726-43*, Yorkshire Archaeological Society Record Series vol.136 (1976)]

Grimston Garth 1788 by Joseph Hargrave (*Dean and Chapter of York/York Minster Library*)

GRIMSTON GARTH

Romantically situated on the crumbling boulder clay cliffs of the Holderness coast, three miles south-east of Aldbrough, Grimston Garth the castellated Gothic house designed and built for Thomas Grimston by the architect John Carr in 1781-6, is set amongst a pleasing and spacious, well-treed landscape.

The Grimston family were settled in the Holderness area from the eleventh century, their former mansion at Grimston, now the site of a farmhouse, being destroyed by fire in the mid seventeenth From 1747 the principal family seat was at Kilnwick-on-the-Wolds. Upon the death of his father John Grimston in 1780, Thomas Grimston conceived the idea of erecting a summer residence where his family could enjoy the pleasures of the sea air and bathing. John Carr, who had previously been engaged in making alterations at Kilnwick, drew up plans for a new house in the increasingly fashionable romantic style of the Gothic revival. Carr's designs were generally in the classic Palladian mode and this more fantastical, asymmetrical edifice was something of a departure for him. The original triangular ground plan with its three rounded corner towers may have been inspired by plans illustrated in *Vitruvius Britannicus* (1771 edn) of Longford Castle, Wiltshire.

Hand in hand with the building of the new house at Grimston Garth came the need to protect this 'summer pavilion' from the often harsh winds, and to surround the place with a landscape in keeping with contemporary taste. The bleak, exposed setting required the planting of trees, shrubs and plants in a natural, picturesque manner, rather than the formal style of the early eighteenth century. To accomplish the landscaping. Thomas Grimston called upon the services of the

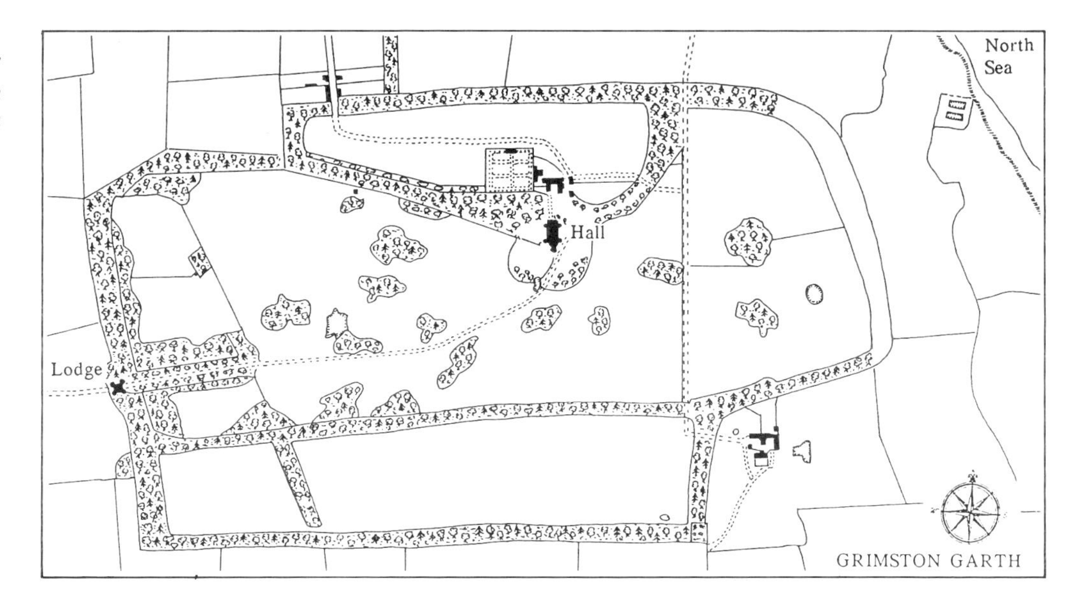

Grimston Garth grounds, **c.***1850, based on the first edition O.S. 6" plan. The trees on the eastern perimeter of the park had been cleared to allow for a view of the sea.*

landscape designer and arboriculturist Thomas White, former pupil of Capability Brown. Parallels can be drawn between Grimston Garth and Strawberry Hill, the Gothic inspiration created by Horace Walpole. Walpole, champion of Capability Brown and the natural in eighteenth century landscape gardening combined a love of the Gothic with an admiration for the 'modern taste' in garden design; when asked if his own garden was to be gothic, Walpole replied: 'You suppose my garden to be gothic too! That can't be: Gothic is merely architecture'.

Although no plan for the landscaping of Grimston Garth survives, a letter from Thomas White to Thomas Grimston dated June 1782 reveals that he had visited the estate and was in the process of drawing up an improvement plan to be delivered in the autumn or early winter. His advice to Grimston included suggestions for preparing a nursery at Kilnwick in which to raise seedling trees, particularly larch, which would then be transported to Grimston for planting out. Considerable planting evidently took place at Grimston, presumably on White's advice, including 6000 oak trees obtained in 1783 from the nurseryman William Reid of Aberdeen. The engraving of Grimston Garth from the south in the late 1780s shows the house set firmly overlooking slightly undulating ground, dotted with clumped evergreens and backed by a belt of trees of apparently mature growth — a certain artistic licence is evident here since planting could have only been very recently completed at this date.

The first edition Ordnance Survey map of 1855 indicates the park at Grimston was clearly landscaped in the natural style; clumps and belts of trees set in and around a large area of grassland, now grazed by cows and sheep. A large walled kitchen garden to the north of the house no longer serves the estate and the ice house, a common feature of so many large estates, is now disused. No other garden features are to be found at Grimston, although a reference exists to a classical temple, designed by John Carr, for the grounds. Thomas Grimston took up residence at Grimston Garth in 1787, however another 25 years passed before the completion of the scheme for the grounds. The large, turreted main entrance gatehouse on the western boundary, completed in 1812, was designed by the architect, Thomas Earle of Hull. The sham portcullis and embattled towers provide an imposing foretaste to the landscaped park and handsome Gothic edifice within. Grimston Garth is the home of Mr. and Mrs. Oliver Marriott and the grounds are private.

[M. E. Ingram, *Leaves from a Family Tree*, 1951; M. E. Ingram, 'John Carr's Contribution to the Gothic Revival', *Georgian Society for East Yorkshire Transactions*, vol.2, pt.3, 1947-8, pp.43-52]

HOLME-ON-SPALDING MOOR

Holme Hall, Holme-on-Spalding Moor, was built for the 4th Lord Langdale in the 1720s to designs by William Wakefield and it was enlarged in the later eighteenth century. The house and grounds lie on the edge of a solitary hill five miles south-west of Market Weighton.

In 1777 Thomas White at the request of Marmaduke, 5th Lord Langdale, drew up plans for improving the grounds which three years earlier had been described by the young Georgina, Duchess of Devonshire as:

> *placed in an absolute bogg in the midst of the Dirtiest and I believe the ugliest part of Yorkshire. It looks Dreary to the greatest degree and what adds to its shocking appearance is a Church all delabre standing with one melancholy stunted tree at the top of a barren hill.*

It appears doubtful that White's scheme for improving Holme was put into effect immediately for the 5th and last Lord Langdale died in April 1778. He was succeeded at Holme by his son-in-law the Hon. Charles Philip Stourton, later Lord Stourton. A neglected Holme Hall was taken over by the Canonesses Regular of the Holy Sepulchre for two years in 1794. By that date some landscaping had seemingly been carried out since 1774 for in describing the grounds around the house a small orchard and a 'shrubbery, above half a mile long' are mentioned. In 1812 John Bigland wrote of the place wanting 'many embellishments of which Nature has rendered it susceptible'; he felt that the estate had distinct possibilities and that 'by a judicious disposition of plantations and walks from the base to the summit of the hill ... it would be easy to form at no very great expense a range of pleasure-grounds, which, in magnificence and picturesque beauty, not many places in England could excel'. The two-acre walled kitchen garden was then described as being entirely overgrown with grass and weeds.

Considerable planting had taken place by the mid nineteenth century when it was said that Holme Hall was 'embellished with pleasure grounds and plantations, extending to the summit of the beacon hill'. The 1st edition Ordnance Survey map of 1855 shows the planting on the ridge extending southwards from the church following closely that suggested on White's 1777 plan, and also a well-treed area to the south and east of the hall known as 'The Park'. Much of this planting remained until after the Second World War. The hall is now occupied by the Sue Ryder Foundation and the former parkland is untreed farmland.

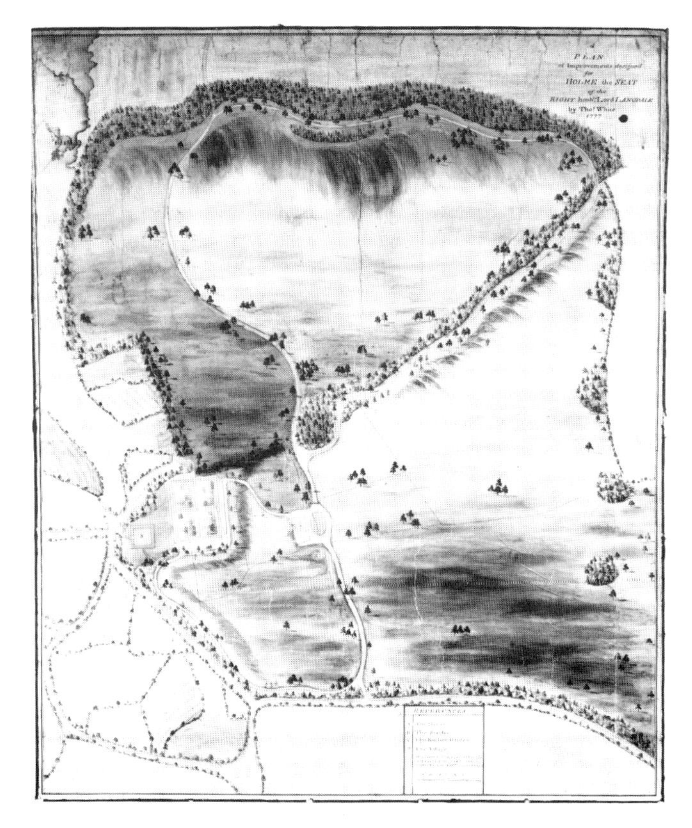

Holme-on-Spalding Moor, improvement plan by Thomas White, 1777 (Humberside County Archive Service)

[K. M. Longley, *Heir of Two Traditions: The Catholic Church of St. John the Baptist, Holme-on-Spalding Moor, 1766-1966*, 1966; D. Neave, *Londesborough*, 1977, p.19]

HOTHAM AND NORTH CAVE

The villages of Hotham and North Cave are linked by parkland which in the eighteenth and early nineteenth century was associated with three properties, North Cave Hall, Hotham Hall and Hotham House. The latter two survive but North Cave Hall which stood to the east of the church was demolished before 1823. The Metham family had a house here from the early sixteenth century and in 1628 Sir Thomas Metham was licensed to empark 500 acres. No park was seemingly made and it was Sir George Montgomery Metham (1716-93) who set about improving the estate and landscaping the grounds around the hall after inheriting in 1763. He promoted a bill for enclosing the open fields of North Cave which was achieved in 1764-5, this included blocking up the road which ran to the north of the church and hall and diverting the Beverley road to its present route to the south. This provided Metham with a suitable area of land to landscape adjacent to the Hall which had previously been hemmed in by open arable fields and the road. The improvements were well under way by 1769 when Metham was paid a visit by the agricultural writer Arthur Young who reported that

> *Sir George assured me, that when he came to his estate, he found his house in the middle of what deserved the name of a bog; the ground all very flat, the offices nosing every window*

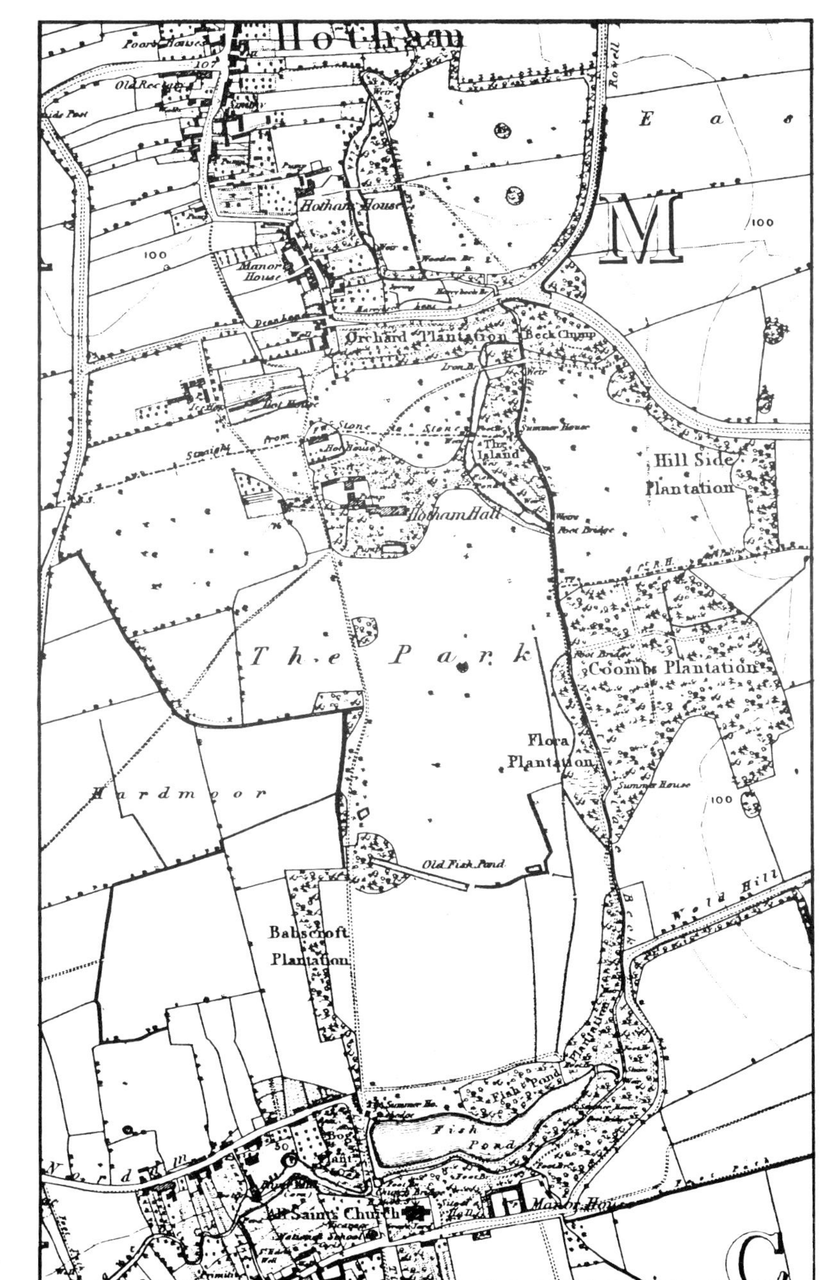

The grounds of Hotham Hall and Hotham House, 1855, from the first edition 6" O.S. plan.

of the mansion, and all in the midst of an open country, with not an acorn planted. His designs are not yet completed but what is done, gives a very pleasing specimen of judgment and taste. Behind the house is an agreeable sloping fall, down to a very fine irregular sheet of water, the banks of which are waved in the truest taste, with a just medium between the slight trivial bend, (which looks like an old streight line turned into a waved one) and the strong, bold, and sudden indentures which should ever be surrounded with natural woods, or wild unornamented ground; a grass-walk waves along the banks, which is close shaven, and kept in neat order, and this is bounded by a thick plantation; so that the whole being in the stile of a pleasure ground, no other plan of forming the water would have had so great an effect. The head at the great end of the water appears at present full in view from both sides; but Sir George designs to give the corner opposite to the house a sweeping wave around the new plantation, which will take off the effect, and be a great improvement; when the plantations get up, the other end will be quite hid, and the whole have no other appearance than that of ornamented nature. Adjoining are many new plantations, sketched with much taste, with zig-zag walks through them in an agreeable stile...

The lake north of the church survives as does Castle Farm which was built in the late eighteenth century as an eyecatcher from either North Cave Hall or, more likely, Hotham Hall. It formerly had an embattled front and an embattled and pinnacled tower.

North Cave, Castle Farm from the west

Metham's improvements were unfinished when in 1773 financial difficulties forced him to sell his North Cave estate to his neighbour Robert Burton of Hotham Hall. Burton or his successor demolished North Cave Hall and merged its grounds with those of Hotham Hall. Hotham Hall which stands in North Cave parish was built by William Burton soon after he purchased the manor of Hotham in 1719. To the south were a series of old inclosures which were seemingly not landscaped until after 1773. They are shown as parkland by 1813 but the landscaping to the north and east of the house had not yet been carried out. The large lake to the east with cascades existed by 1827.

Further north a similar serpentine lake provides the major feature in the pleasing landscaped grounds of Hotham House which were probably laid out in the early nineteenth century by James Whyte. Whyte had inherited through his wife the house and 30 acres which had been sold in 1772 by Sir George Montgomery Metham to her brother the Rev. Richard Gee.

The grounds of Hotham Hall, and Hotham House are private.

See colour plate p.45

[See Arthur Young, *A Six Months' Tour through the North of England*, 1770, vol.1, p.166; K. J. Allison, *Victoria County History, East Riding*, vol.4, pp.21, 23-4, 118]

HOUGHTON HALL, SANCTON

Houghton Hall, two miles south of Market Weighton, was built around 1765 for Philip Langdale to the designs of Thomas Atkinson of York 'an able architect in both Gothic and classical styles'. Its simple Georgian style in pale pink brick with a pediment and two wings linked by quadrant walls, harmonises well with its splendid 'natural' landscape setting.

The grounds 'disposed with great taste and judgment' were laid out to a design of Thomas White dated 1768, after the completion of the new house. The plan, very similar in conception to the one White drew up for Norton Place, Lincolnshire, in 1772, shows an L-shaped area in dotted lines to the south-east of the new house, most probably the original house. White's plan diverted the existing road from the south to an easterly approach. A serpentine lake some fourteen acres in extent to the south of the house, was formed by damming the stream from Coldwell Spring and was bisected by a cascade taking the water down to a lower level. The whole design was serpentine in character, gentle and sinuous; it incorporated a curving ha-ha between the house and south lawn while the north lawn was circumscribed by a walk through the orchard and tree belt.

A large kitchen garden, well screened from the house by plantations, stands to the west. The view to the south with its typical parkland planting of clumps, belts and individual trees extends out to rising farmland, which could be reached by a footbridge over the cascade. The farm at the edge of the parkland was provided with battlements, named Castle Farm, and made a feature in the landscape.

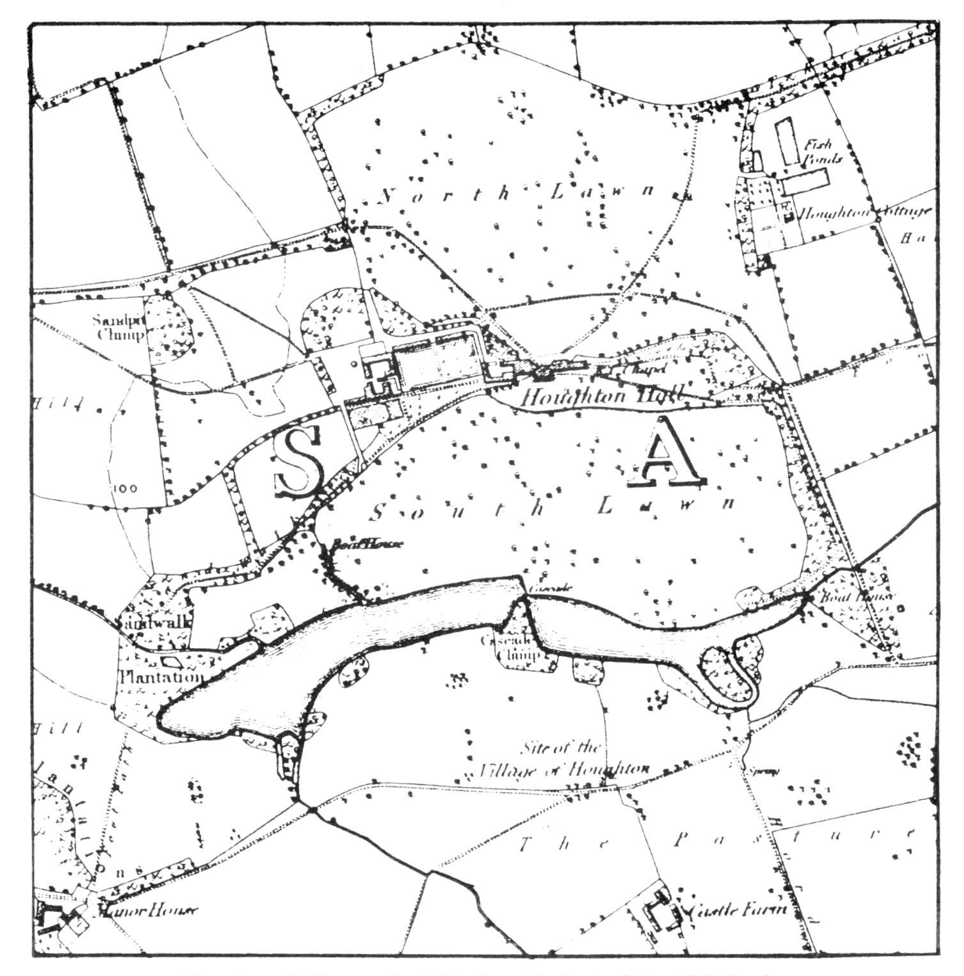

Houghton Hall grounds, 1855, from the first edition 6" O.S. plan.

The large and flourishing trees including oaks, limes, chestnuts, copper beeches and walnut make Houghton one of the best preserved examples of Thomas White's landscape in the style of Capability Brown. In the later nineteenth century a formal terrace with symmetrical flower beds and a sundial was laid out between the house and the ha-ha.

Houghton Hall is the home of Lord and Lady Manton and the grounds are private.

[A. Oswald, 'Houghton Hall, Yorkshire' *Country Life*, 23 & 30 December 1965]

Houghton Hall from the south viewed across the lake

Houghton Hall, improvement plan for the grounds by Thomas White, 1768 (Lord Manton/Hull University Photographic Service)

Houghton, the parkland from the south east 1992 (*Ed Dennison/Humberside Archaeological Unit*)

The grounds of Birdsall House, c.1760
(Lord Middleton/Hull University Photographic Service)

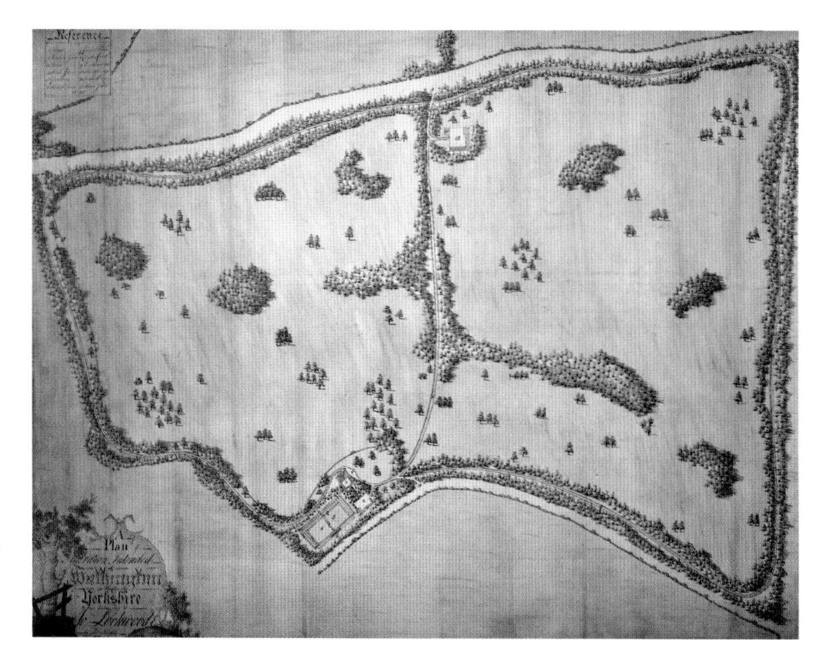

Walkington Lodge (later Hall), plan for alterations to the grounds by Adam Mickle for John Lockwood 1803.
(Hull University Photographic Service, reproduced by permission of Hull University Archivist)

Sir George and Lady Strickland in the grounds of Boynton Hall, 1751 by Arthur Devis (Hull Museums and Art Galleries)

HOWSHAM

Howsham Hall is splendidly placed alongside the River Derwent seven miles south-west of Malton. This fine stone house built around 1610 by William Bamburgh is set in a landscape created by the Cholmley family from the mid eighteenth century. A series of plans made in 1705, 1758, 1776 and 1792 and a birds-eye view of the house and grounds in 1718 enable the various changes to the grounds to be charted.

A reconstruction of the layout of the grounds around 1720 shows a typical early eighteenth century formal garden. To the north east of the hall were a series of rectangular walled enclosures. Immediately adjoining the house was a square enclosure comprising a large garden of four symmetrical parterres. To the south were an orchard and kitchen garden. Further east another larger formal garden was again divided into geometric beds possibly with low box hedges. The main axis was provided by a central pathway which led from the east front of the house through the two walled gardens and into a long avenue flanked by a double row of trees. Between the avenue and the River Derwent was a plantation cut through with diagonal walks.

By 1758 considerable changes had taken place possibly begun by Nathaniel Cholmley who inherited the Howsham and Whitby estates in 1755. The formal gardens had been swept away to the east of the hall and the grounds extended immediately to the south. The latter involved the demolition of half-a-dozen houses and was the first stage in the reduction of the village which then comprised two rows of houses on either side of a green built upon at its northern end.

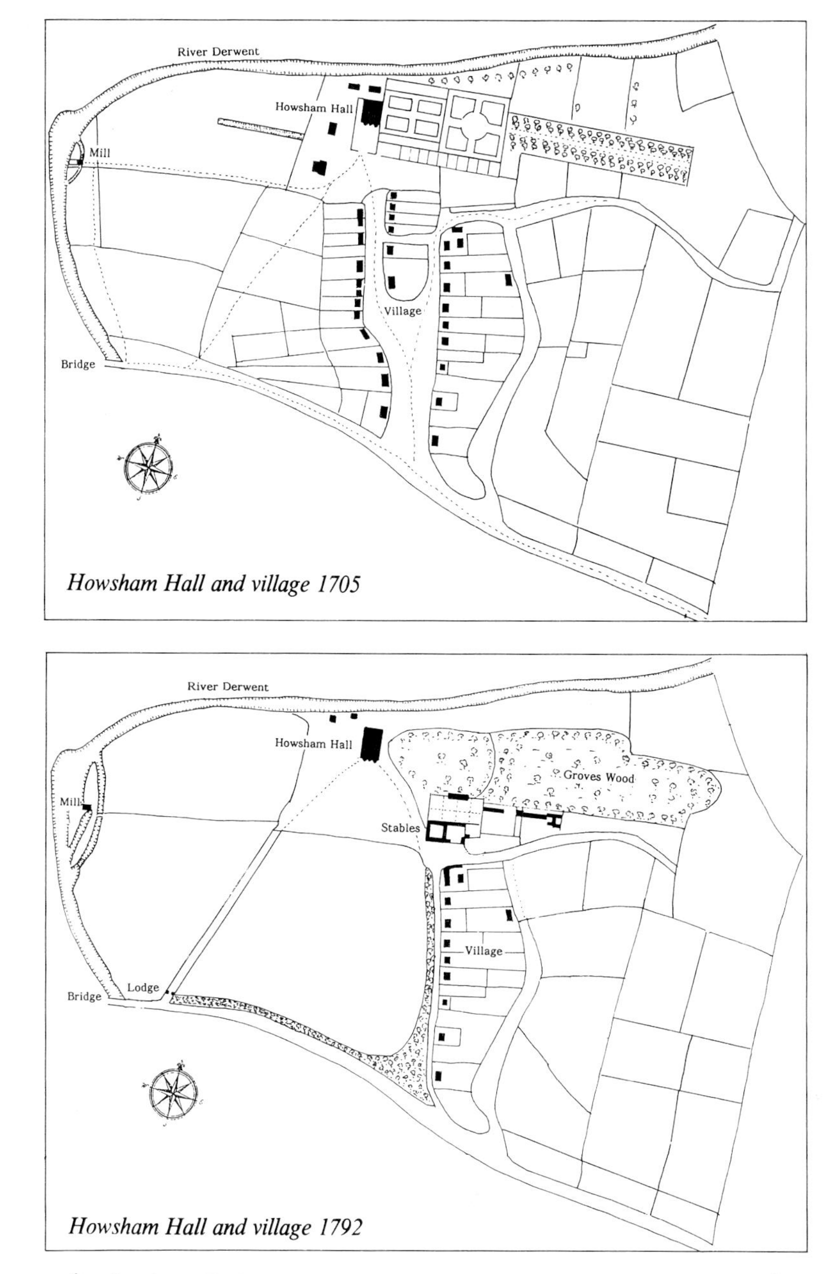

Howsham Hall and village 1705

Howsham Hall and village 1792

(based on plans at Humberside County Archive Office and North Yorkshire County Record Office)

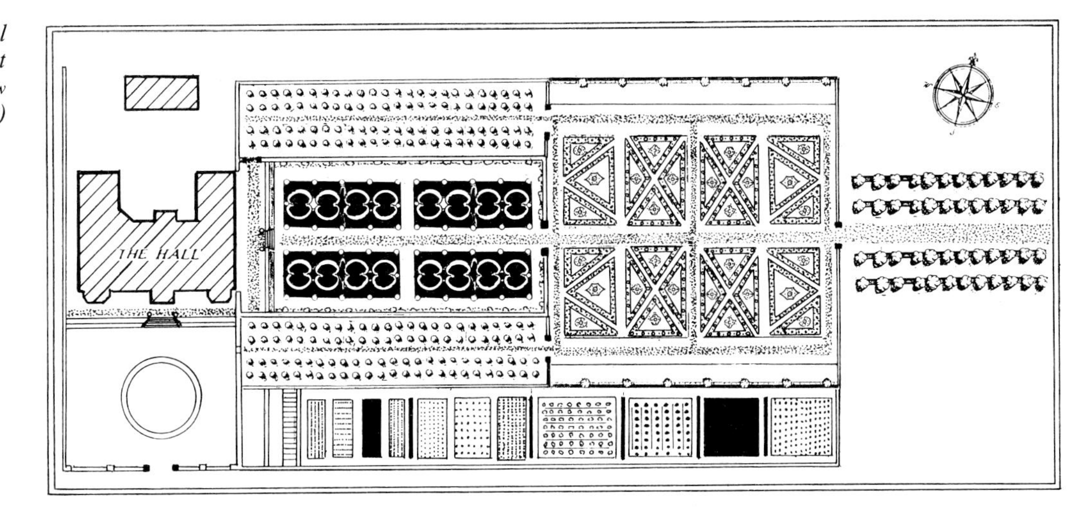

Howsham Hall. Conjectural reconstruction of garden layout c.1720 (based on plans of 1705 and a view of 1718)

Around 1770 Cholmley set about modernising the interior of the hall with the advice of John Carr who undoubtedly designed the stable block. About the same time Capability Brown was consulted and, although no details are known, it is likely that he was responsible for the 'improvements' made to the landscape by 1776. The whole of the western row of houses was demolished and their sites and the former village green were taken into the grounds and planted up with a belt of trees. The area westwards from the village to the Derwent was planted as open parkland with belts of trees sited on the northern and southern boundaries. A lodge was built near Howsham Bridge and a carriageway built across to the hall. The water-mill on the Derwent was Gothicised, possibly to designs by Carr, as a feature in the landscape. Between 1776 and 1792 the final stages in the transformation, from formal to informal landscape, took place with the planting out of the long avenue and the clearance of the plantations between it and the Derwent.

In 1783 Elizabeth Montagu writing to the Duchess of Portland described her stay in the 'Elysian fields' of Howsham:

> *The view from the windows is very pleasing; you behold a navigable river gently gliding through a green valley adorned with fine trees, and the prospect is much enlivened by barges continually passing ... Mr. and Mrs. Cholmley ... have built a village very near their house, and fitted up and furnished the houses with all the decent comforts humble life requires ..*

Howsham Hall is now a preparatory school and the grounds are private.

[Plans in North Yorkshire County Record Office ZCG, and HCAO; A. Harris, *The Rural Landscape of the East Riding of Yorkshire 1700-1850*, 1961, pp.76-7; A. Oswald, 'Howsham Hall', *Country Life*, 24 & 31 August 1935, pp.194-9, 220-5; B. English, *The Great Landowners of East Yorkshire 1530-1910*, 1990, p.216]

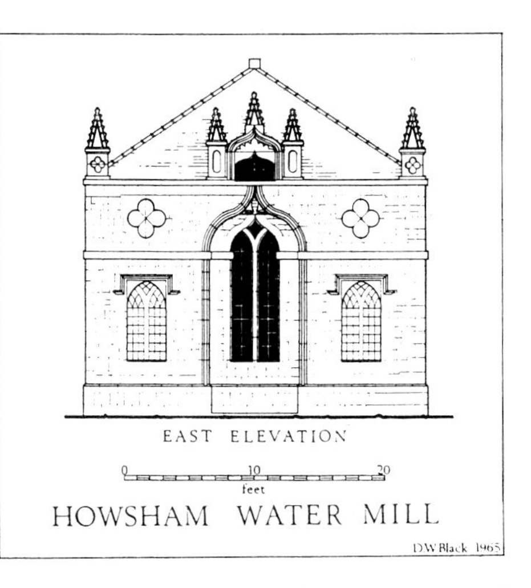

Howsham, Gothic water mill, reconstruction of east elevation by D. W. Black, 1965

Burton Constable Hall from the east, **c.***1680.*
(Burton Constable – Leeds City Art Gallery)

Burton Constable Hall from the east, 1777, by George Barrett.
(Burton Constable – Leeds City Art Gallery)

Hotham Hall in the mid-nineteenth century from the north-east by R. B. Harraden.

KILNWICK HALL, KILNWICK-ON-THE-WOLDS

Kilnwick Hall, five miles south of Driffield, was described in 1828 as 'a handsome mansion ... pleasantly situated on the banks of a stream near the village' with 'a considerable quantity of wood, as well as some extensive pleasure-grounds around it'. The house was demolished in 1951-2 and little remains to indicate the former presence of the gardens, successively formal and informal, associated with it.

Thomas Grimston (1702-51) inherited the Kilnwick estate from a relative, Admiral Medley, in 1747. The charming 'Prospect of Kilnwick Hall' in 1750 reconstructed by Francis Johnson from a contemporary sketch and a plan by John Lund shows the house in a formal setting. Immediately south of the house is a formal fishpond which leads into an avenue lined with double rows of trees running down to the road. On the east side are shown two walled enclosures containing the kitchen and flower gardens.

John Grimston who succeeded in 1751 continued with the improvements to the house and gardens begun by his father. It was he who employed John Carr to carry out considerable alterations to the house in the years 1769-74. Carr's gate piers survive, those at the south entrance flanked by the remains of an 18th century ha-ha. By 1785, the whole formal garden, already slightly modified by 1776, had been swept away, replaced by an informal park dotted with clumps of trees and protected along the east and west boundaries by undulating plantations. A walled kitchen garden was laid out some distance to the east of the house between 1776 and 1780 and was approached by serpentine walks.

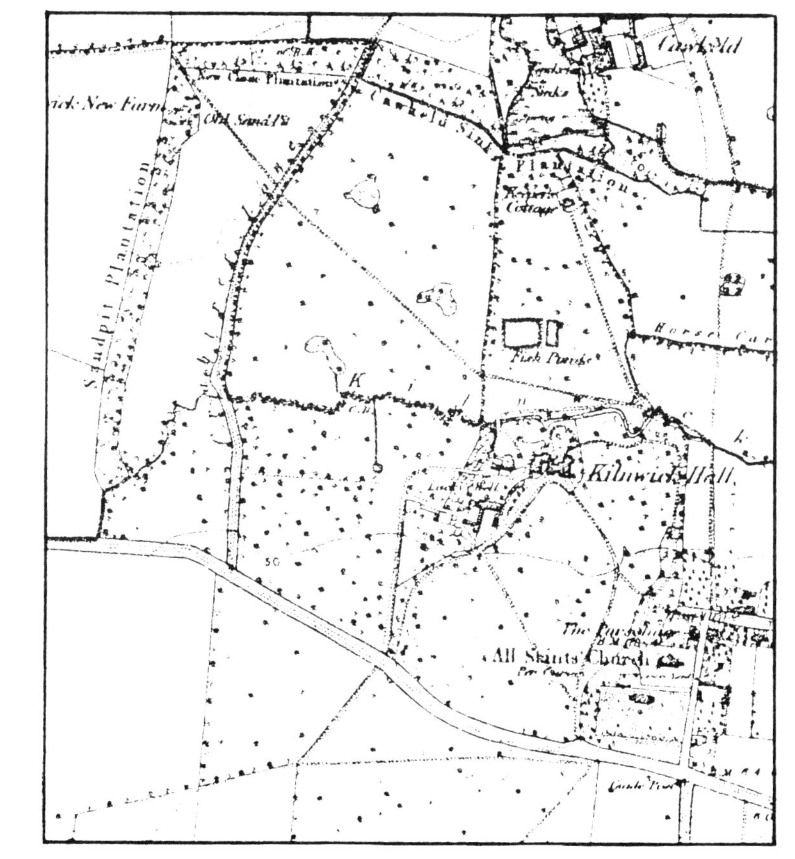

Kilnwick Hall grounds, 1855. from 1st edition 6" O.S. plan.

Although no improvement plan for the layout of the park exists, it is possible that Thomas White may have been involved. He prepared a plan for Grimston Garth in 1782 and may well have been called upon to advise at Kilnwick in conjunction with John Carr's work there in the 1770s. The surviving correspondence of John Grimston with nurserymen, Telfords of York, Perfects of Pontefract and others, demonstrates his enthusiasm for tree planting and gardening. Another correspondent on the subject of trees and shrubs was Thomas Knowlton, the botanist and gardener at Londesborough and William Pontey (d.1831), distinguished nurseryman, writer and expert on forest trees, was for some years head gardener at Kilnwick.

[HCAO DDGR; M. E. Ingram, *Leaves from a Family Tree*, 1951.]

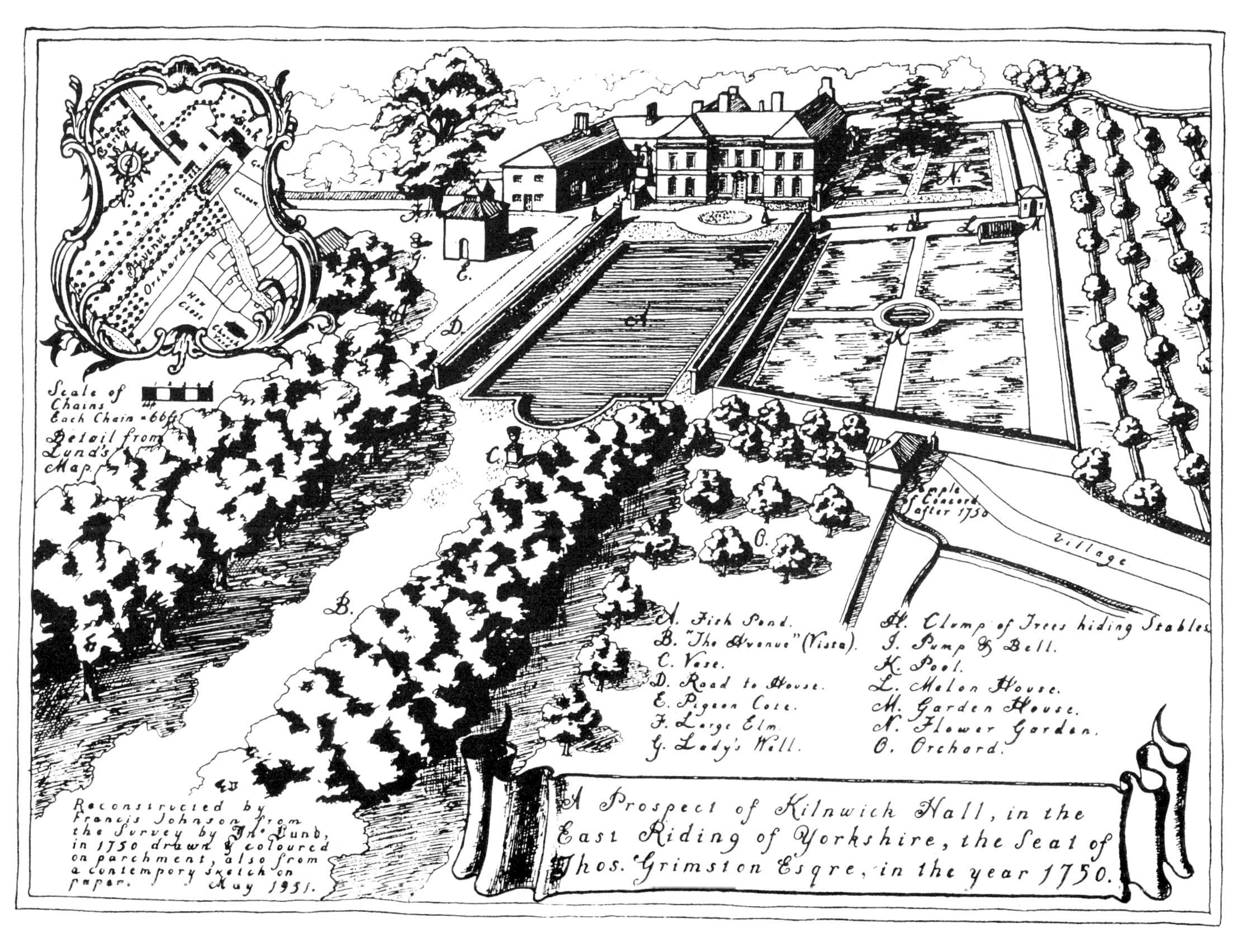

Kilnwick-on-the-Wolds. A reconstruction of the gardens as they were around 1750 by Francis Johnson, from M. E. Ingram, Leaves from a Family Tree, *1951*

Londesborough, view from the terrace across parkland towards Easthorpe (Hull University Photographic Service)

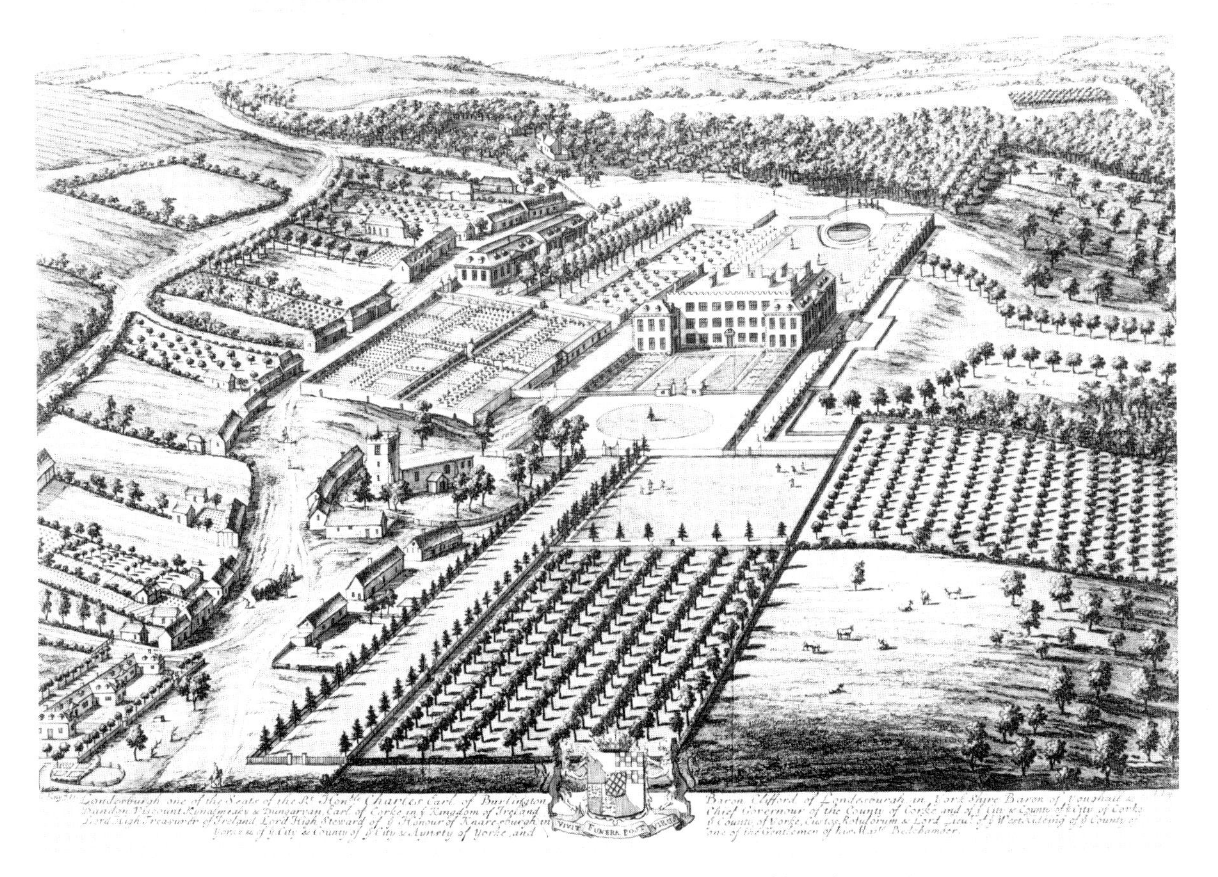

Londesborough, c.1700 by Leonard Knyff, engraved by Johannes Kip

LONDESBOROUGH

At Londesborough on the western edge of the Wolds, two miles north of Market Weighton are the remnants of the East Riding's most important eighteenth century landscaped park and gardens. Important because they were largely created by Richard, 3rd earl of Burlington a major figure in the history of gardening. In 1704 Burlington, then nine-years old, had inherited the family's vast estates in Ireland, Yorkshire and Middlesex. His main residences were Burlington House in Piccadilly and Chiswick House in Middlesex, but almost every year from 1720 to his death in 1753 some time was spent at his northern retreat at Londesborough. Here each autumn he regularly escaped from his role as a great patron of the arts and followed the more rustic pursuits of hunting and shooting.

The house and grounds that Burlington inherited at Londesborough are shown in a fine birds-eye view of c.1700 by Knyff. The three-storey Elizabethan house built by Francis Clifford, later 4th Earl of Cumberland, had been greatly enlarged with the addition of 'wings' to the north and south, by the 1st Earl and Countess of Burlington around 1680. It was Lady Burlington, daughter and heiress of the 5th Earl of Cumberland who was seemingly responsible for the laying out of the modest formal gardens which surrounded the house. The diary of Robert Hooke, scientist, architect and secretary of the Royal Society reveals that he was the designer of these gardens in 1676-7.

It was a difficult site on which to lay out such a formal garden for the house stood on a comparatively restricted area of raised ground which fell sharply away to the south-east. In order to provide a level site the ground to the east of the hall was raised behind a fine arched terrace wall. This happily survives as does the impressive flight of stone steps leading from the terrace into the park. These features can be clearly seen on Knyff's birds-eye view which shows the area to the east of the hall as a lawn embellished by five statues with a raised terrace on three sides and a circular pond with a fountain creating an apsidal eastern end to the gardens. To the north of this apse a triangular 'bastion' jutted out into the park.

To the west of the house the gardens were divided into a series of rectangular enclosures. A recently planted avenue, presumably the one of yews which still remains, led up to the house. To the south of this avenue was a bowling green laid out in 1678-9 with formal plantations to the south and west. To the north of the house were the walled kitchen garden, an orchard and the stables. Knyff's view shows little of the parkland except a semi-circle of trees leading into a wide avenue to the south of the terrace and another avenue leading eastwards through a plantation. Deer and cattle are shown within the park.

It can be safely assumed that these modest formal gardens underwent no great alteration before Lord Burlington

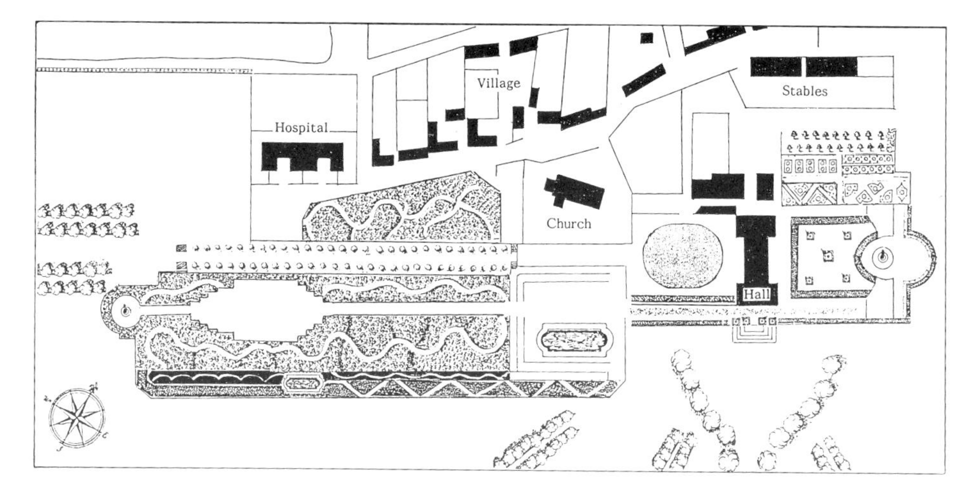

Londesborough Hall, plan of pleasure grounds based on plan of 1739

inherited in 1704 and almost certainly little was done before the 1720s when the progress on his better known works at Chiswick made it possible for him to turn his attention to his northern seat. Payments for work in the park and gardens at Londesborough rise substantially after the appointment of THOMAS KNOWLTON as gardener late in 1726. Some £1600 was spent on labourers in the park and gardens in the years 1728-32. In June 1730 Knowlton complains of being 'exceedingly engaged with workmen of every kind' and that Burlington, whom he terms 'our great and best of Lords', was coming down on purpose to see the alterations he had made 'which are more within these six months than all the four years before'. Such activity continued with Knowlton reporting to a friend in July 1738 that he was 'now in my greatest hurry having better than 40 people to govern and take care of'.

The work carried out in these years is documented by estate accounts, the correspondence of Knowlton and Burlington, a descriptive poem 'Lanesborough Park' by Mr. Wyld of Otley published at York in 1738 and a fine estate plan drawn up by Thomas Pattison in 1739. The plan shows the park and garden as seemingly in a state of transformation from a formal to a more natural style. Many elements of the formal grounds can still be seen but meandering walks and irregular areas of water, cascading to a large 'natural' lake, have been introduced, and in the more distant part of the park are shown clumps of trees.

To the east of the hall the gardens remained unaltered but to the west they have been transformed. The yew avenue was retained but to the north a 'wilderness' area with winding walks, terminating in small open spaces with features such as vases or statues, was

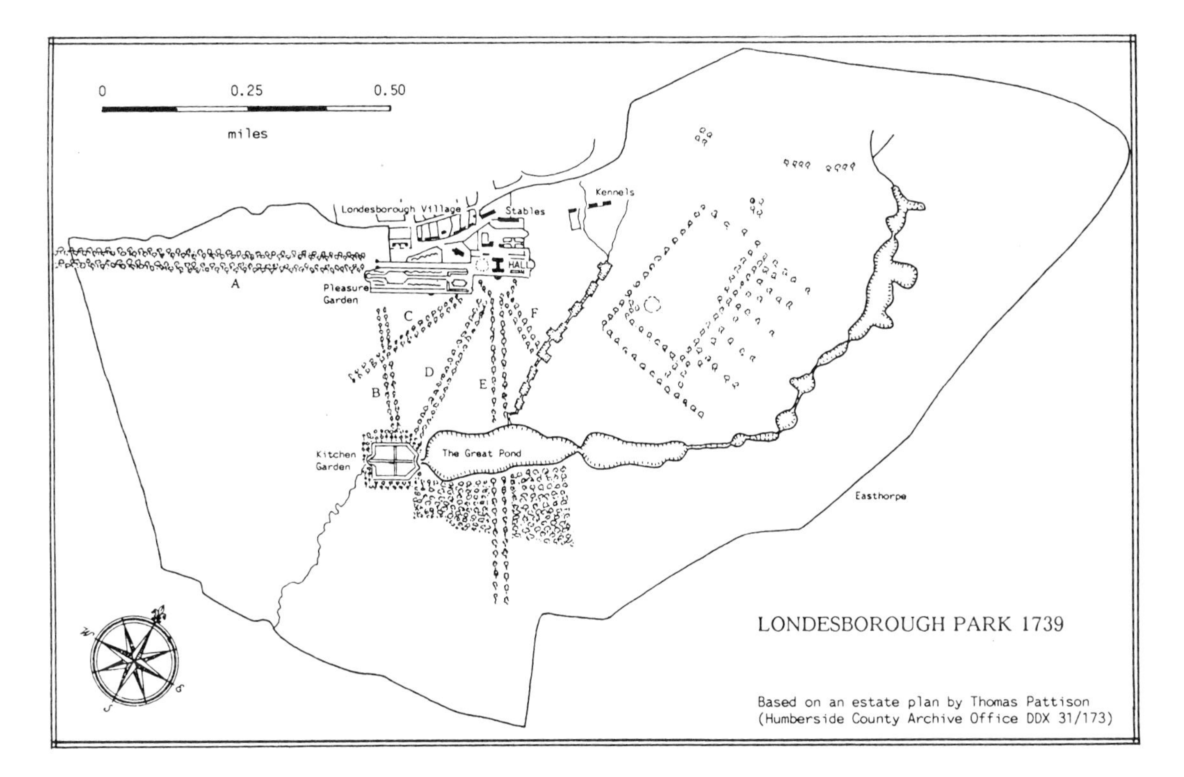

created by the demolition of the houses and cottages to the west of the church and the extension of the gardens to the village street. South of the avenue the bowling green was replaced by a rectangular pond with apsidal ends from which ran a formal walk which expanded in stages to form a large open area and then contracted to a walk again and ended in a circular clearing. One of these spaces was filled by Burlington with great urns. Wyld's poem speaks of 'a beauteous Wilderness', 'a cool grove', a 'gay Alcove', and 'a wandring Labyrinth ... to no one form the several openings lead ... so rude it seems, yet must by Art be wrought'. This Rococo pleasure garden was echoed by that which still survives at South Dalton nearby.

Westwards from the pleasure gardens a broad avenue was planted running over a mile to the York road. Begun in the 1720s it was probably not completed until the early 1740s when permission was sought from Sir Marmaduke Constable of Everingham to continue it across his land to the main road. The avenue ran through land that was added to the park in the late 1730s. Burlington greatly enlarged the park which had covered some 230 acres in 1724. A modest addition of 38 acres was made in 1729 then ten years later some 400 acres of agricultural land to the south and west of the existing park and much of the hamlet of Easthorpe were emparked. This involved the demolition of five houses.

It is this enlarged park that is shown on Pattison's plan of 1739. The semi-circle of trees and wide avenue [E on redrawn plan] running south from the house remained from the late 17th century layout but a further four avenues have been planted. Two [C-D] run south-west, and one [F] south-east from the house, the fourth [B] goes from the west end of the pleasure gardens to the newly sited kitchen garden. Remnants of avenues B, C and D survive, C being largely of walnut and B and D chiefly of Turkey oak which is said to have been introduced into England in 1735. It has been suggested that its use at Londesborough was owing to Knowlton's links with the botanist William Sherard who had been British

Londesborough, the long avenue from the south west 1992 (E. Dennison/Humberside Archaeological Unit)

consul at Smyrna in Turkey.

Two series of ponds or lakes are shown on the 1739 plan, the largest group consisting of eight irregularly shaped lakes which cascade down from the north-east corner of the park to a large nine-acre lake adjoining the new kitchen garden. This surviving series of lakes, which Knowlton termed canals, were constructed 1728-30. In excavating the great lake a Roman road was discovered which attracted the attention of antiquarians including Dr. Francis Drake from York and William Stukeley. The smaller group of more rectangular ponds running into the great lake from the north are a puzzling feature and may have been associated with the necessary drainage works undertaken in the late 1730s. These no longer exist.

The kitchen garden was moved from north of the house to its new four-acre site in the valley to the south-west in about 1730. The surviving garden walls were built in 1732 and in 1735 Lord Burlington provided plans for the fine rusticated stone gateway on the north side. In the north-west corner a greenhouse and hothouses were built where Knowlton kept his collection of 'innumerable rare and exotic plants' which the antiquarian William Stukeley noted in 1740. In the hot houses Knowlton successfully cultivated guavas, melons, pawpaws, pomegranates, orange and lemon trees and above all pineapples. The pineapples which were regularly sent to Lord Burlington in London were also distributed to favoured local gentry. A plan of the kitchen gardens made in 1792 shows a series of dwarf walls on which were trained Muscadine and Burgundy vines, plum trees, and white currants. Peaches, nectarines, apricots, pears, cherries, plums and grapes were grown on the 11ft high garden walls. In the garden Knowlton also grew the 'new' strawberry, a recently introduced ancestor of the cultivated garden strawberry. The stream running through the garden abounded in water-lilies.

Improvements in the park were continued in the 1740s and early 50s. In October 1746 Burlington writes of making 'great progress in the water, which will really have a good effect' and in the winter of 1750-51 Knowlton was much engaged in planting. In March 1751 he was planning the laying out of rides or walks through the thorns in the Ox Close on the west side of the park so that it would 'have a Garden look, as having a little Art mix'd with Nature, so that the one beautifies the other'.

On the death of Lord Burlington in 1753 his estate passed to his son-in-law William Cavendish, marquess of Hartington who succeeded as 4th Duke of Devonshire in 1755. Although during the next 90 years Londesborough was only visited occasionally by members of the Devonshire family the pleasure gardens were kept in excellent order even after the demolition of the hall in 1818-19. The

Londesborough, gateway at the kitchen garden designed by Lord Burlington, 1735. (Neil Thwaites)

Londesborough, the parkland from the south 1992, the great lake and kitchen garden in the foreground. Notice the remnants of the avenues in the park.
(E. Dennison/Humberside Archaeological Unit)

Londesborough, the terrace c.*1900* (*Hull University Photographic Service*)

park however was turned over to farming and the large lake drained. In 1839 a shooting lodge was built in the park some distance from the old hall site. The estate was sold in 1845 to George Hudson, the 'Railway King' and then in 1849 to Lord Albert Denison who was created Lord Londesborough. He and his descendants made periodic use of the house for shooting parties and they restored the pleasure gardens, refilled the great lake and resuscitated the kitchen gardens.

A vivid picture of the park and gardens at the very end of the nineteenth century is provided by Sir Osbert Sitwell in the first volume of his autobiography, *Left Hand, Right Hand*! Sitwell's mother was the daughter of the second Lord Londesborough. The present owners of the estate Dr. and Mrs. Richard Ashwin have done much to conserve what remains of the late seventeenth and early eighteenth century park and gardens and their son Anthony is actively restoring the lakes and cascades.

The house site and gardens are private but public footpaths, including the Wolds Way, cross the parkland.

[see David Neave, 'Lord Burlington's park and gardens at Londesborough, Yorkshire', *Garden History*, 8, Spring 1980, pp.69-90; Blanche Henrey, *No ordinary gardener: Thomas Knowlton 1691-1781*, British Museum (Natural History), 1986.]

RISBY

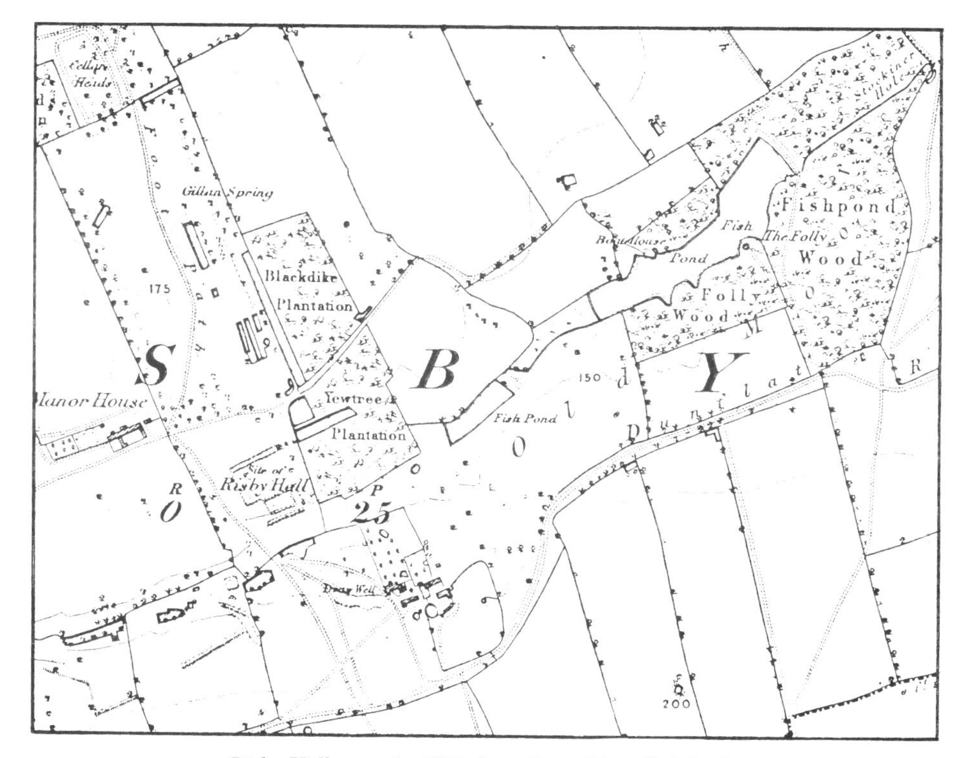

Risby Hall grounds, 1855, from first edition 6" O.S. plan.

At Risby, three miles south-west of Beverley, can be seen the well-preserved earthworks of a late seventeenth century Italianate terraced formal garden associated with a house that was demolished 200 years ago. In 1540 Sir Ralph Ellerker had a house and deer park here where he entertained King Henry VIII. This house which stood in the area known as Cellar Head was replaced on a new site in the 1680s by the house associated with the formal garden. This was built for Sir James Bradshaw of Bromborough, Cheshire who had married the heiress to the Ellerker estates.

An undated early eighteenth century print of Risby provides an excellent representation of the house and the terraced garden that was laid out about 1684. Four flights of steps link the terraces and to the left and right two small brick pavilions stand on pyramidal earthworks overlooking the elaborate parterres on two levels. The gardens are surrounded by a high brick wall which at the southern end becomes a low wall with railings bowed to accommodate the geometric-shaped pond with an ornate central fountain. Today the terraces remain intact and a rather decayed pond retains the broad outline of its more formal predecessor.

Plans were made in the late 1760s by Eaton Mainwaring Ellerker (c1722-71) to destroy these formal gardens. Arthur Young who stayed with Ellerker in 1769 described the setting of Risby Hall and reported in detail on the improvements proposed.

> *The house, which is a large quadrangle with three fronts, is situated on the brow of a rising ground ... a winding valley runs before the south front, at the distance of 2 or 300 yards, the banks of which are fringed with spontaneous thorn trees. To the north is a large lawn surrounded with plantations; to the north west, but unseen from the house, is a middling sized park, all hill and dale, and wood, exceedingly beautiful; near the house to the east, are several groves of young timber... Mr. Ellerker proposes to throw down the fences of the inclosures between the park and the house, so as to join it on one side to the garden. The valley ... is to be floated with water, and will then have the appearance of a very noble irregular lake, winding both to the right and left into a wood ... old garden walls (will be) thrown down, and all obstructions removed, so that the lake may be seen from the house ... the water, when the sun shines on it, will appear through the trees in the most picturesque manner ... From the house will be seen, over the lake, some fine irregular slopes scattered with a few trees and thorns, rising to a plantation of firs, which, when somewhat altered, will have a very elegant appearance. Embossomed in their centre is to rise a little Grecian temple, just showing its dome among the trees.*

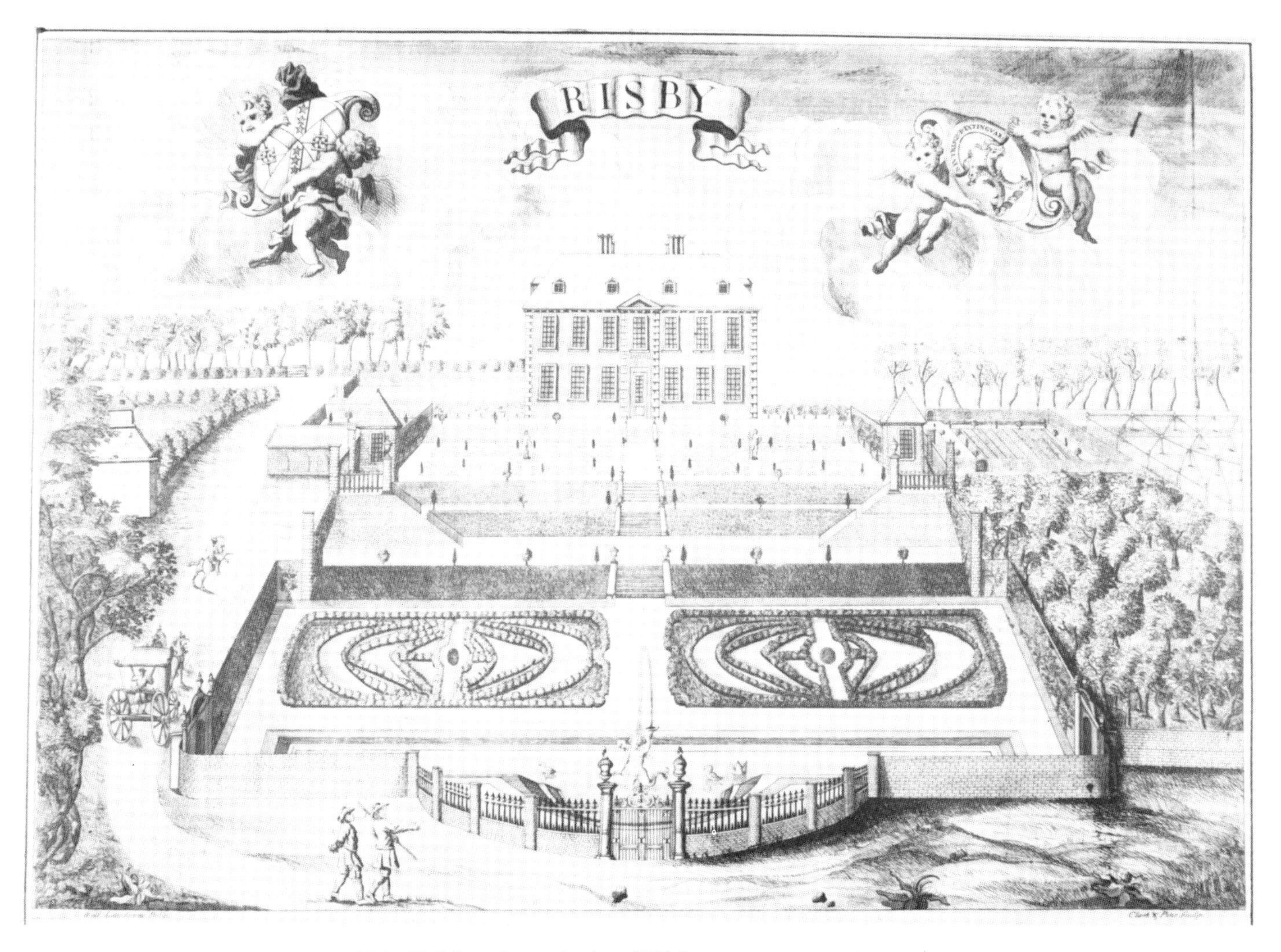

Risby Hall from the south, about 1700 (*Wakefield Art Gallery and Museums*)

Little progress was probably made with these improvements before the deaths of E. M. Ellerker in 1771 and his son and heir four years later. However to the south east in the valley are two ponds presumably the remnants or forerunners of the 'noble irregular lake' which was to have extended along the valley. Beside the larger pond is a tall octagonal Gothic folly.

Risby Hall suffered two disastrous fires in the 1770s-80s and it was subsequently demolished. The house site and ponds are on private property and are not accessible but the terraces can be clearly seen from the public road near Risby Park Farm.

(D. Neave, 'Risby Hall', *Georgian Society for East Yorkshire Newsletter,* 7, 1980; S. Neave, *Medieval Parks of East Yorkshire,* Hutton Press, 1991, pp.46-7]

Risby from the west, 1992, showing the garden terraces to the left foreground and deserted village earthworks flanking the farm on the right.
(E. Dennison/Humberside Archaeological Unit)

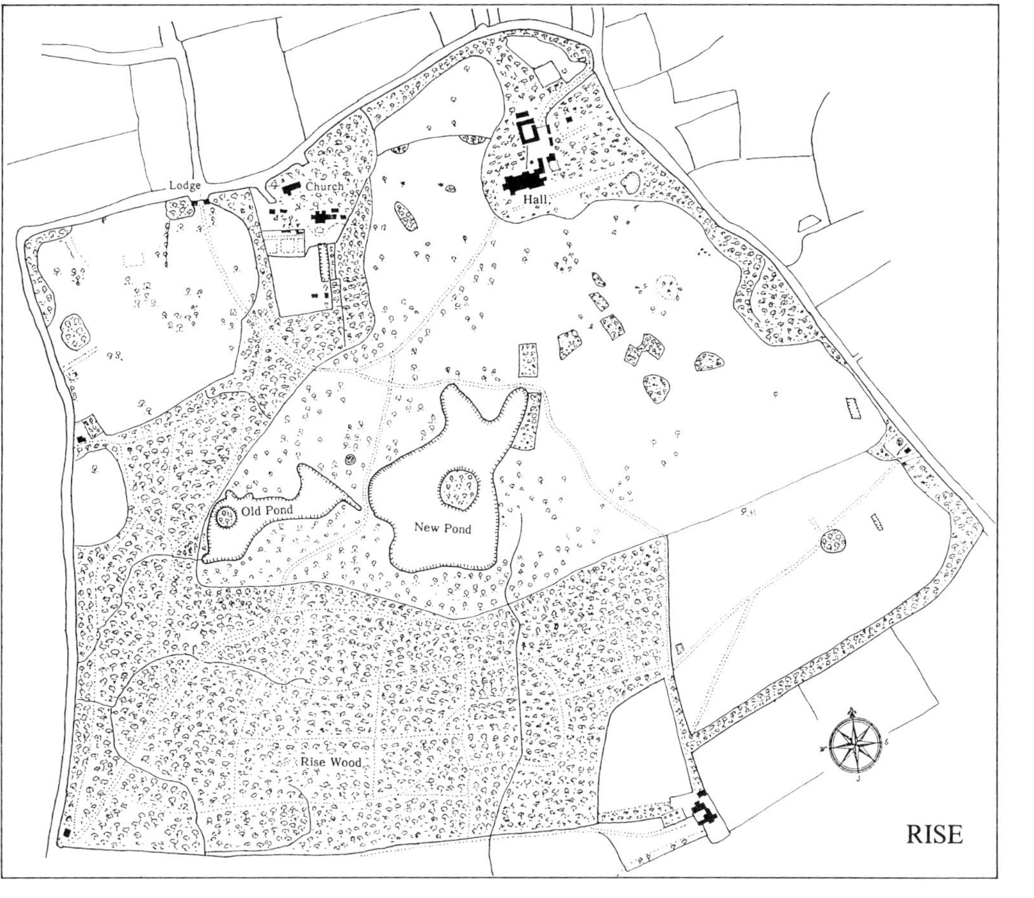

Rise, the parkland 1855, based on 1st edition O.S. plan.

RISE

Rise, five miles south-west of Hornsea, has one of the few areas of ancient parkland in Holderness; there was a deer park there in 1228. The estate has been owned by the Bethell family since the early seventeenth century. A plan of 1716 shows that the park then lay to the south of the hall which stood in modest formal gardens. Within the wooded parkland there were clumps of trees and a large irregular pond. From the pond, which may have partly served as a decoy, an avenue of trees led north-west through Blackhall or Lodge field.

In 1773 William Bethell refronted the hall and in 1775 obtained from Capability Brown 'A General Plan for the Alterations of the Place'. The plan which does not survive is only referred to in Brown's account book and it is not known to what extent the improvements carried out followed his instructions. The first edition 6″ Ordnance Survey plan of 1855 shows major changes having taken place since major changes having taken place since Jefferys' survey of 1772. In 1772 the area to the south of the hall was divided into two with woodland to the west and a fenced deer park to the east. Within the park there appears to be an avenue running southwards. Plans were presented at the East Riding Quarter Sessions at Christmas 1775 seeking a diversion of the highway. Not long afterwards some 40 acres of Rise Wood were cleared and taken into the park. Within this newly cleared area was sited a large irregular

Rise, the park from the west, 1989 (*E. Dennison/Humberside Archaeological Unit*)

pond, termed the New Pond in 1855, while to the west the smaller Old Pond remained. Both had circular islands. Clumps of trees were dotted throughout the enlarged park and along the boundaries on the eastern side plantations were made. Meandering walks were cut through the substantial remains of Rise Wood on the western side.

Some of these changes which had taken place by 1827-9 may have resulted from alterations that took place when Rise Hall was rebuilt 1815-20. The park has changed little since 1855 and looks exactly as one would expect a mature Capability Brown landscape to appear.

The grounds, owned by R. A. Bethell, are private.

[See Susan Neave, *Medieval Parks of East Yorkshire*, Hutton Press, 1991, pp.32, 48-9.]

Thorpe Hall grounds, **c.***1850, based on first edition 6″ O.S. plan.*

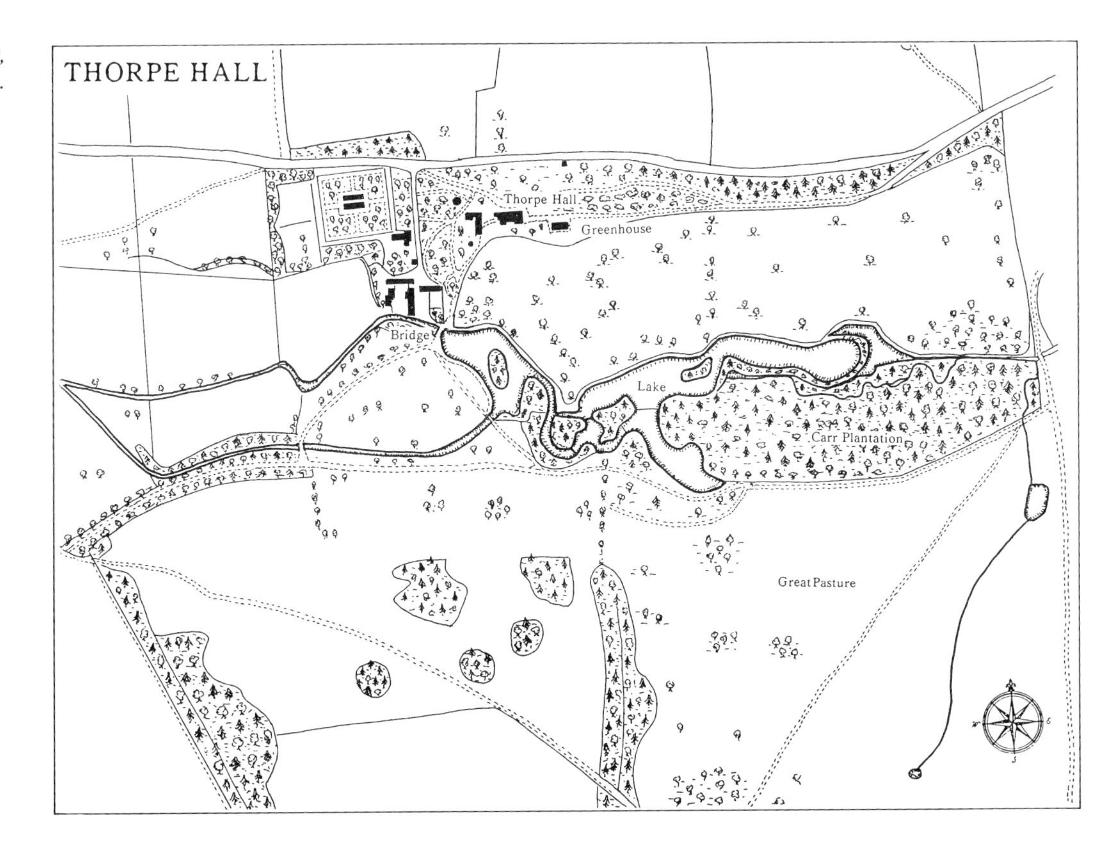

RUDSTON, THORPE HALL

The grounds of Thorpe Hall, Rudston, four miles west of Bridlington, with large serpentine lakes, ornamental buildings and extensive planting, are a fine example of a picturesque Regency landscape design as advocated by J. C. Loudon.

Thorpe Hall was probably built by Thomas Hasell soon after he inherited it c.1695. The house was remodelled and enlarged in the middle and later eighteenth century and in 1886 a large block was added on the west side. There is no record of the appearance of the gardens in the eighteenth century although a letter from Mrs. Greame of Sewerby, dated 16 July 1779, records: 'We dined at Thorpe, where we met the officers and most of the neighbours in a magnificent Roothouse; walked in a Grove which was illuminated in the manner of Vauxhall'.

It was Godfrey Bosville, later 3rd Lord Macdonald, who inherited Thorpe in December 1813 and lived there from the following year until his death in 1832, who undertook the major landscaping of the grounds. The Upper Pond is said to have been dug in 1815, to give much needed employment at the end of the Napoleonic Wars, and the larger Lower Pond was made or enlarged in 1830. The ponds are ornamented with several wooded islands and miniature waterfalls. The contemporary three-arched Stable Bridge at the western end of the Upper Pond is faced with sea-eroded stone from Filey Brigg.

Of particular importance at Thorpe is the charming series of early nineteenth century ornamental garden buildings. The hexagonal wooden dovecot, raised on brick pillars, and topped by a cupola had sadly deteriorated beyond repair and has gone but the octagonal timber-built game larder, the dairy, and the billiard

The Dairy, 1821, at Thorpe Hall, Rudston (*Hull University Photographic Service*)

room and greenhouse, all built around 1821, remain. The dairy is a Grade I listed building and is an outstanding example of a model dairy in the rustic picturesque style. It is an elongated octagon surrounded by a verandah and internally it retains the original Regency fittings including decorative wall-tiling and stained glass windows representing the Four Seasons. The billiard room and greenhouse or orangery lie some distance to the east of the hall. These simple classical buildings, seen prominently on the mid-nineteenth century watercolour are a major component of the picturesque landscape at Thorpe.

Thorpe Hall is the home of Sir Ian and Lady Macdonald and the grounds are private.

(G. Wood *Historic Homes of Yorkshire*, 1957, pp.123-7; Alice, Lady Macdonald *The Fortunes of A Family*, 1928, pp.122-3)

(see colour plate p.71)

SCAMPSTON

Scampston Hall, situated six miles south-east of Malton in the Vale of Pickering, is set in a superb landscape of more than local interest because of the involvement of the two most important landscape designers of the eighteenth century.

The manor of Scampston was acquired in 1610 by William Hustler, a wealthy Bridlington draper, and sold in the early eighteenth century to Sir William St. Quintin of Harpham, the 3rd baronet (c.1660-1723). A new house was erected at this time and alterations made to the exterior in the 1750s by the 4th baronet and again in the 1770s by the 5th baronet. In 1803 Scampston Hall was considerably altered to the designs of Thomas Leverton to produce the house we see today.

Both Charles Bridgeman and Capability Brown were involved with the design of the gardens and park, and a 1787 description of the park records the magnitude of the task:

> *the difficulty of rendering so dead and untractable a plain, beautiful, has been here gradually surmounted; and if you remark how flat and hungry a level Scampston House is built on, it will be allowed, there are not many inland places in the kingdom, so situated, whose improvements have such an agreeable effect on the passenger.*

Plans for creating a formal garden at Scampston Hall were drawn by Charles Bridgeman about 1730 and although no trace of this garden now remains, there is some evidence that Bridgeman's plans were implemented. An estate map of 1766 shows formal plantations in the south-east corner of the park cut through with

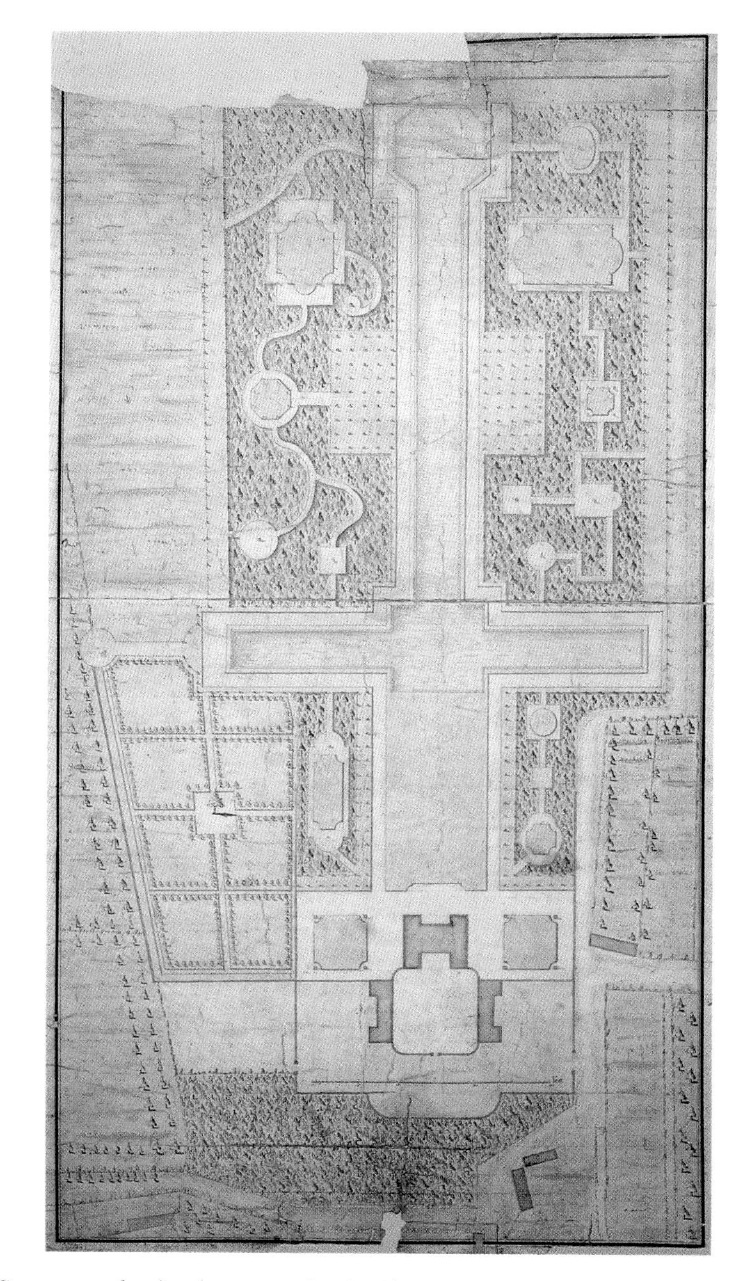

Scampston, plan for pleasure gardens by Charles Bridgeman c.1730 (Bodleian Library)

Scampston, three watercolours by Francis Nicholson, c.1780.
(Hull University Photographic Service)

The Palladian bridge

The Gothic tea house or deer lodge.

The cascades.

straight rides leading to circular clearings in the style of Bridgeman. In 1736 the 4th baronet had the main York-Scarborough road diverted to the south presumably to allow him to carry out his landscaping plans.

Bridgeman's plan shows a formal layout with a complicated water system running on a north-south axis from the house; a T-shaped lake and octagonal pool are flanked by rectangular plantations of trees, that on the left incorporating straight edged walks and groves, while the other shows winding, more curvilinear forms.

No formal water garden exists although Scampston boasts three connected lakes, probably created in the late 1730s, which feature in fine views from the house to the southern boundaries of the estate. The 4th Baronet (1700-1770) was much interested in the improvement of the estate and in the years 1751-66 he employed as his gardener William Speechley, later to gain fame as head gardener to the Duke of Portland at Welbeck, Nottinghamshire, and as the author of treatises on hot house plants, stove designs and tree planting. At Scampston Speechley had followed Robert Teesdale who had gone to be gardener at Castle Howard.

Sir William St. Quintin, the 5th Baronet, succeeded in 1770 and in the same year called upon Capability Brown for plans and advice on improvements. Brown produced designs for the Palladian bridge at the head of the water and for the cascade built in 1775; he also advised St. Quintin on widening the lake and creating a sunken fence bordering the main road. The plan by Page of 1829 shows a typically Brownian landscape with clumped planting, a ha-ha in front of the house, sinuously curving lake and broad areas of lawn. The house was altered at this time with the addition of square 'Palladian' turrets, a favourite detail employed by Capability Brown, to the top of the projecting wings, suggesting that Brown had a hand in the architectural designs.

Scampston Hall grounds, 1829, based on a plan by Edward Page

A Gothic-style tea house or deer lodge situated on the far side of the A64 was completed in about 1768 and forms an impressive eyecatcher viewed from the house. Stylistic and documentary evidence suggest a design by the architect John Carr who produced similar park buildings at Sledmere and Barnsdale.

A large four acre kitchen garden located north of the house included hot houses for the cultivation of pineapples and other exotic fruit, and records also indicate the existence of a menagery in the mid eighteenth century.

A balustraded terrace and flower garden with sundial were created in the early twentieth century by William Herbert St. Quintin who succeeded to Scampston in 1876. A naturalist and ornithologist of great repute, he formed a fine collection of birds and waterfowl; he was also a keen cultivator of orchids and grew alpine plants in a rock garden built by Backhouse of York.

Scampston Hall is the home of Mary, Lady Legard St. Quintin and the grounds are private.

[HULL DDSQ; A. Oswald, 'Scampston Hall, Yorkshire', *Country Life*, 1 & 8 April 1954; D. Stroud, *Capability Brown*, 1975, pp.173-4.]

SLEDMERE

In 1812 John Bigland wrote:

> *Sledmere may be considered as the ornament of that bleak and hilly district [the Wolds]. The circumjacent hills are adorned with elegant farmhouses ... in summer the waving crops in the fields, the houses of the tenantry elegantly constructed and judiciously dispersed, the numerous and extensive plantations skirting the slope of the hills, and the superb mansion with its ornamental grounds in the centre of the vale, form a magnificent and luxuriant assemblage little to be expected in a country like the Wolds; and to a stranger on his sudden approach the coup d'oeil is singularly novel and striking.*

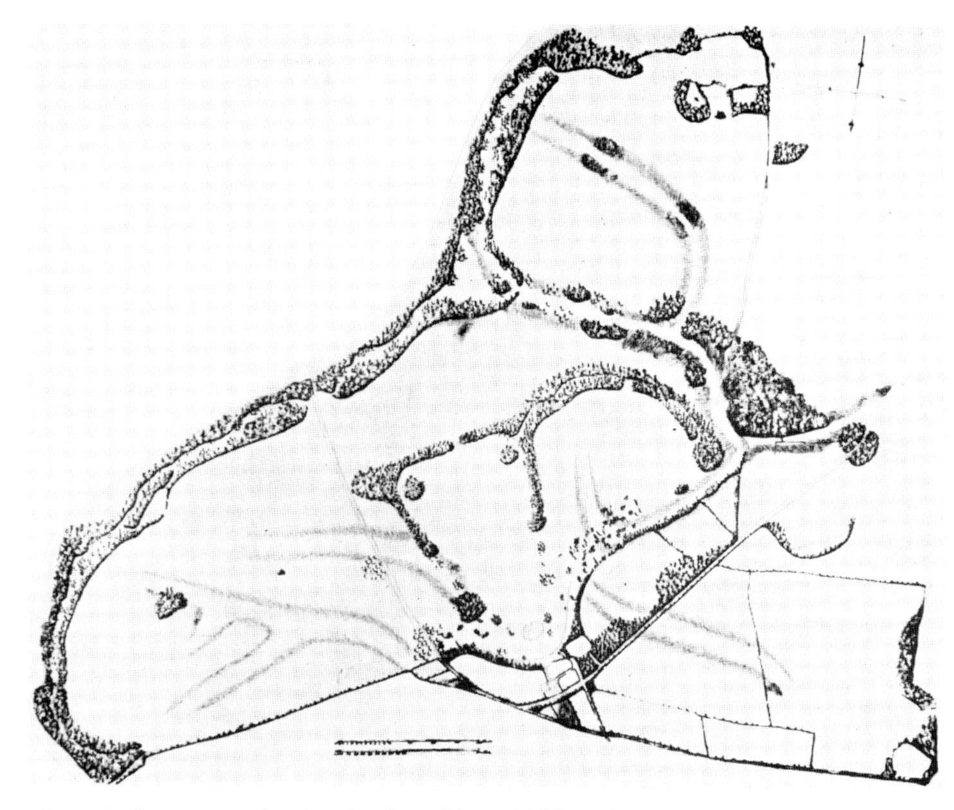

Sledmere, improvement plan by Capability Brown, 1777 (Sir Tatton Sykes)

When in 1751 Richard Sykes (1706-1761) laid the foundation stone for his new house at Sledmere it was very much within the village, near to the church with farmhouses and cottages close by. In order to improve its setting he seemingly blocked roads, demolished houses, and made a lawn flanked by two plantations which diverged to form The Avenue which was terminated on the high ground to the south by a further plantation at right angles. An undated and unsigned plan survives to show the intended layout near to the house which included what appears to be a huge circular pond to replace the village mere, and to the west a straight walk cut through a plantation led from the house to a circular clearing with an octagonal summer house or temple in its centre.

This rather restricted layout was clearly seen by the young Christopher Sykes (1749-1801) as being in need of improvement when he was granted possession of Sledmere by his ageing father in 1770. A survey of the parish was made in 1774 and the following year an act of Parliament was passed facilitating the enclosure of the open fields of Sledmere, which also included provision for diverting the main Bridlington to York road to the north of the house. Sykes then began his transformation of the landscape. In December 1775 he commissioned Thomas White 'who lays out pleasure grounds and rides' to draw up proposals for improvements. White's plan dated 1776 covered a large area and provided his usual solid planting belt along the boundaries with plantations along the valleys and on the prominent ridge in the middle foreground with a scattering of clumps of trees in the parkland. The Avenue and remaining village houses were entirely eliminated. Seemingly dissatisfied with White's proposals Sykes secured the services of 'the Great Brown' who visited Sledmere in September 1777 and again a year later. Capability Brown's plan prepared by November 1778 covered the more immediate area to the house and basically it differed little from White's except that it showed that he intended not to remove the trees from the southern part of the Avenue. Neither plan was followed exactly for Sykes seemingly used elements from both as guides to his grand planting scheme.

Sykes planted more than one thousand acres of land, purchasing larch, Scots pine, beech and other trees from Thomas White at Retford and the nurserymen Perfect and Telford. Between 1771 and 1800 Sykes spent at least £8,648 on planting and in the six months ending April 1779 alone a total of 177,210 trees was planted.

In addition to planting Sykes also introduced numerous strategically placed farm and other buildings on the estate many to his own design including Marramatte and Life Hill Farms, the deer house and the elegant greenhouse erected near the house in 1786. The last was demolished in the 1850s as was the ice house designed by John Carr. Castle Farm also by Carr is the most distinctive of the buildings in the landscape. An octagonal walled kitchen garden was built to the east of the house with a row of four gardener's cottages alongside.

Other than changes made to the grounds immediately around the house in the twentieth century the landscape at Sledmere today is very much what was intended by Sir Christopher Sykes and his advisers over 200 years ago. The memorial erected to Sykes in West Heslerton church by his daughter after his death in 1801 claims that he transformed the countryside around his estate 'from an open sandy barren extensive sheepwalk, comprising several thousand acres, into well cultivated farms adorned with plantations which from their vast extent have since assumed the appearance of forest'.

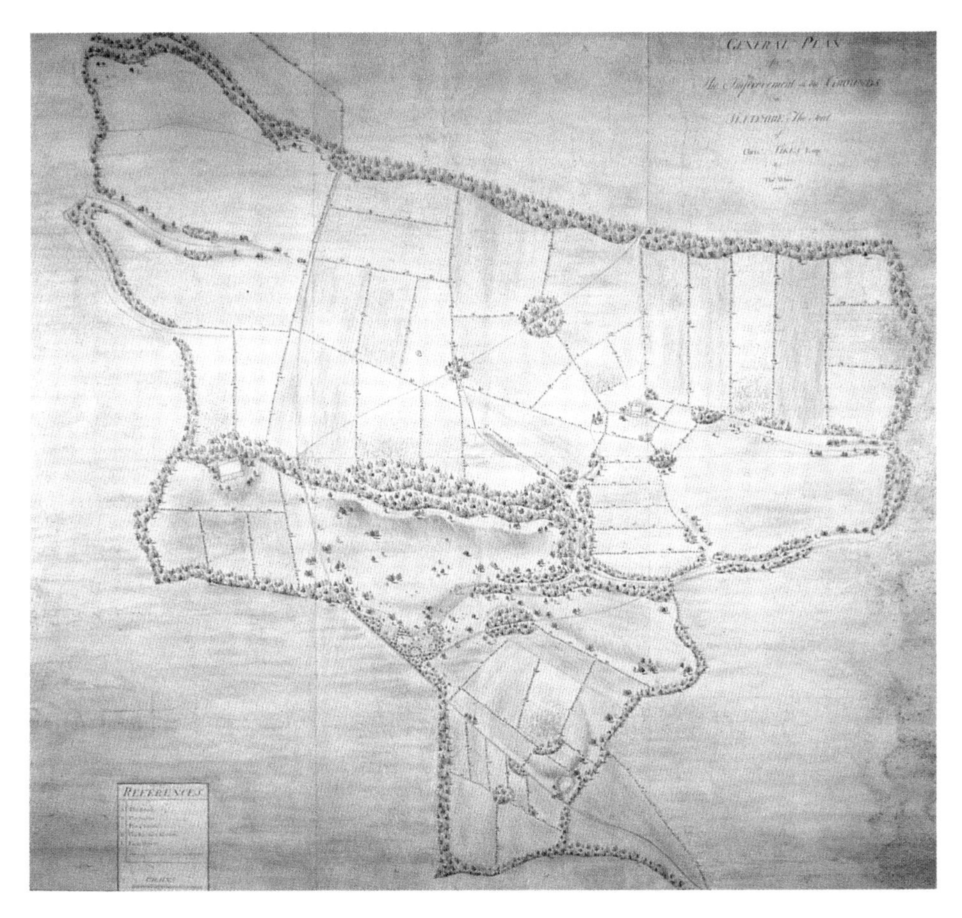

Sledmere, improvement plan by Thomas White, 1776
(Sir Tatton Sykes/Hull University Photographic Service)

Sledmere Hall is the home of Sir Tatton Sykes. The house and part of the grounds are open in the summer months.

[HUL DDSY; Plans at Sledmere House; J. Popham, 'Sir Christopher Sykes at Sledmere', *Country Life*, 16 & 23 January, 1986, pp.128-32, 188-191]

Sledmere House from the south west by Thomas Malton about 1795, showing the Orangery
(Sir Tatton Sykes)

Sledmere from the south east looking up The Avenue
(Hull University Photographic Service)

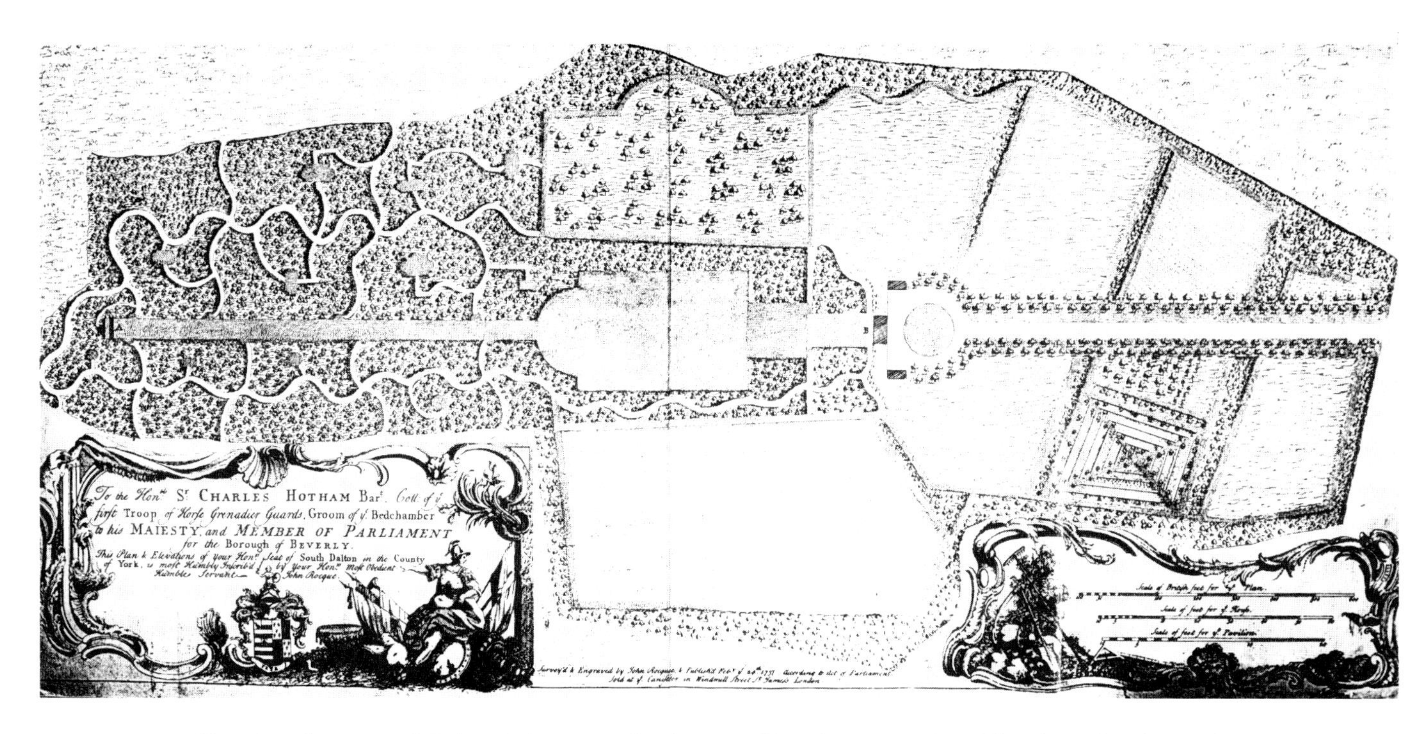

Plan of gardens at South Dalton, 1737, surveyed and engraved by John Rocque (from Vitruvius Brittanicus, *vol.4)*

SOUTH DALTON

Dalton Hall, at South Dalton, five miles north-west of Beverley, the home of the Lord and Lady Hotham, has one of the best preserved early eighteenth century Rococo gardens in the country. The estate has been in the hands of the Hotham family for over 300 years. When Sir John Hotham, 2nd baronet (d.1689) purchased the Manor of South Dalton in 1680 it comprised little more than 200 acres of land. The principal holding was the manor house and 107 acres of old enclosed land surrounded by open arable fields to the west of the village.

Following the destruction by fire of the main family residence at Scorborough in 1705-6, Sir Charles Hotham, 4th baronet (d.1723), had a splendid house, designed by Colen Campbell, built in Eastgate, Beverley 1715-21. However on succeeding in 1723 Sir Charles, 5th baronet (d.1739) abandoned the Beverley house and seemingly decided to reside at South Dalton when in East Yorkshire.

The well known engraving by John Rocque of the house, pavilion and grounds at South Dalton, dated 24 February 1737 shows that Sir Charles had ambitious plans for his estate. There is no evidence that the house, a fine Palladian villa, was built or that work had even commenced on it at the time of Sir Charles' death in January 1738 but the grounds to the west of the intended house were laid out as shown and the pavilion built. The architect of the house and pavilion are unknown but they have been attributed with some confidence to both Colen Campbell and his former assistant Roger Morris. Another possible candidate is Richard, 3rd earl of Burlington, a close friend and neighbour of Sir Charles Hotham. There are numerous links between Burlington and Hotham, indeed their wives were cousins. In August 1725 the estate steward at Holme-on-Spalding Moor reported to his employer that 'The Earl of Burlington and his lady hath been three weeks at Lounsbrough ... I believe Sir Charles Hotham has been there most of the time.'

South Dalton from the east, 1992
(E. Dennison/Humberside Archaeological Unit)

Dalton Hall from the west looking along the walk (Hull University Photographic Service)

Thorpe Hall, Rudston from the south showing billiard room and orangery on the right. Water colour of about 1850.
(Sir Ian Macdonald/Hull University Photographic Service)

Estate accounts show that money was being spent on the house and grounds at South Dalton from 1723. By the end of 1736 Hotham had spent £930 on the house and stables and £1660 on the gardens, the latter includes £294 for 'the garden seat at the end of the wood' which was built in 1733-34. The garden seat or pavilion was probably inspired by the York Watergate in London, then attributed to Inigo Jones. It is very similar to the gateway that Colen Campbell designed for Burlington House. The pedimented facade with its attached columns with vermiculated rustication was built of Roche Abbey stone purchased in 1733-4. William Kent produced a much more ambitious design for a garden seat or temple for Sir Charles Hotham which was published around 1733 in Isaac Ware's *Designs of Inigo Jones and Others*, but not executed.

Even if Lord Burlington was not the architect of the house and pavilion at South Dalton his advice would almost certainly have been sought and his gardener, Thomas Knowlton, did play a major part in the design of the grounds which have marked similarities to the gardens then being laid out at Londesborough. On 24 August 1729 Knowlton informed a fellow botanist, Samuel Brewer, that he had 'waited on the Honbl. Sr Charles Hothom & spent most of the afternoon with him about a new designe for a garden & paddock &c.' The following November he reports being at 'a gentlemans seat ...on account of measuring his grownd for a new disigne for a garden & paddock & shall be that way againe within a month'. This would seem to be South Dalton where the head gardener from 1728, John Scott, a subscriber to Philip Miller's *Gardeners*

South Dalton. Elevations of the garden seat or pavilion as built and the intended house, 1737, by John Rocque.

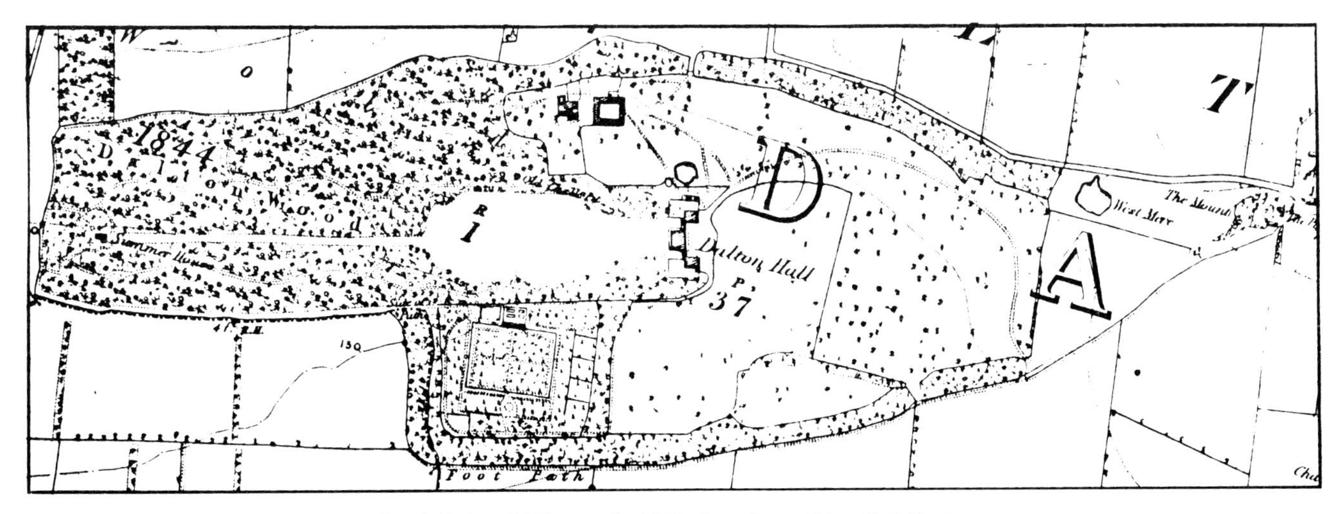

South Dalton Hall grounds, 1855, from first edition 6" O.S. plan.

dictionary, 1731, became a close associate of Knowlton.

Although a considerable number of trees were purchased from nurserymen at York and London, including the garden designer Stephen Switzer, the western third of the proposed grounds was already well established woodland in 1723. Immediately to the west of the site of the proposed house was created a vast lawned area which opened out in three stages before curving in to lead into a long yew-lined walk up to the 'garden seat'. On either side of the walk meandering paths in the woodland led to a whole series of small regular clearings. To the east of the house site, on a line with the garden walk, was proposed a double avenue of trees cutting through existing fields. It is not known how much of the proposals for the eastern half of the grounds was carried out although a kitchen garden was built where planned in 1737. This adjoined the old manor house from which in 1772 a road lined with trees led to the pleasure gardens.

The manor house was seemingly demolished once the present house, built to the designs of Thomas Atkinson, was ready for occupation in 1776. It was at this time that the grounds on the eastern side were probably landscaped in the natural style. At some date between 1807 and 1852 the kitchen gardens were moved to their present site to the south of the great lawn.

Beaumont, 3rd Lord Hotham (d.1870) greatly increased his landholding in South Dalton at the enclosure of the open fields in 1822-7. This enabled the 5th Lord Hotham (d.1907) when he was altering and enlarging the house in 1872-6 to increase the size of the park and gardens from just over 100 acres to 400 acres. The new parkland the formal terraced garden immediately to the west of the house were laid out to designs by the landscape gardener William Broderick Thomas who was also working then at Sandringham. In the 1880s Thomas laid out the grounds at the nearby Bishop Burton Hall.

Fortunately neither in the 1770s nor 1870s were any major changes made to the grounds to the west and although now less formal in appearance and without the serpentine walks there still survives what Giles Worsley has described as 'the bones' of a most important Rococo garden.

The grounds at South Dalton are not open to the public.

[HUL DDHO; G. Worsley, 'Rococo Survival' *Country Life*, 17 May 1990, pp.198-200; W. A. Eden, 'South Dalton' in H. Colvin and J. Harris (eds.), *The Country Seat*, 1970, pp.117-120.]

WELTON

The villages of Welton and Melton are situated about nine miles west of the city of Hull not far from the banks of the Humber, commanding fine prospects across the estuary. Such a site proved attractive to eighteenth century Hull merchants wishing to reside away from the close built town and both villages were surrounded by the 'Arcadian walks, woods, and lawns' of several modest but elegant mansions.

The largest was Welton House, which prior to its demolition in 1952, was a well known landmark north of the A63 which cut through the surrounding parkland. A house, belonging to James Shaw, was first recorded there in 1748 and upon his death in 1768 the property was devised by him to Thomas Williamson, a member of an important family of Hull merchants. Williamson set about improving the house and its grounds and in 1769 obtained a design for the landscape from Thomas White.

White's plan shows the main road from Melton to Welton prior to its diversion intersecting the estate. A sunken fence runs in a partial circle to the south of the house giving a view across the lawn which was to be well planted with clumps and individual trees. The boundaries of both the south and north lawns are shown planted with belts of trees, gaps allowing views south across the Humber. A slightly winding walkway followed the line of the tree belts with seats placed in carefully selected positions. The enclosure of Welton open fields in 1772-75 allowed Thomas Williamson to acquire additional land to the south and east of his grounds and incorporate them into his landscaped park.

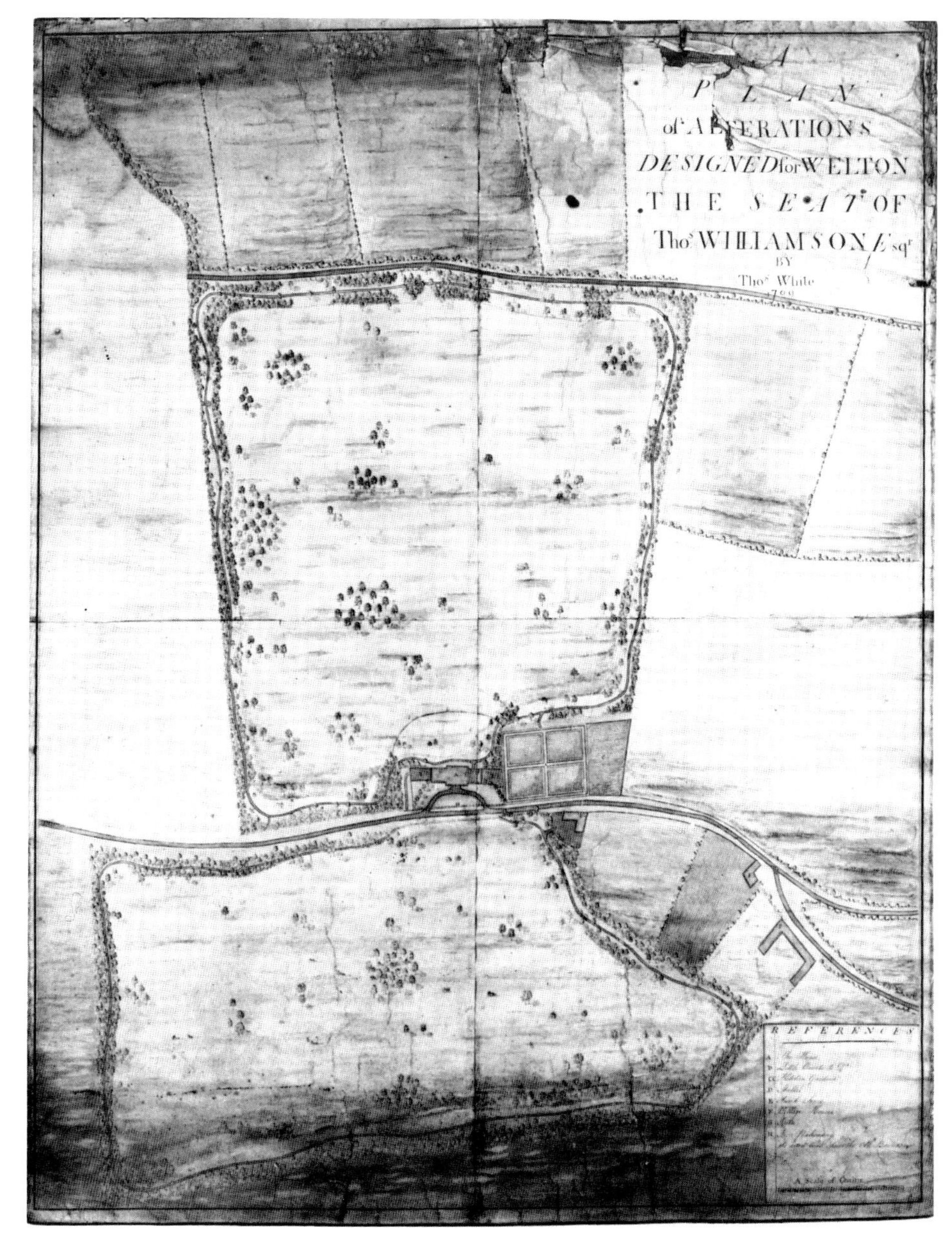

Improvement plan for the grounds of Welton House by Thomas White 1769
(Humberside County Archive Service)

Prior to 1772 both Welton and Melton were described as 'very bare of wood', however Thomas Williamson and his brother, Joseph, who owned the adjoining Melton Hill estate planted extensively and transformed the landscape. Joseph was awarded a gold medal by the Society of Arts in 1772 for the planting of 8000 English elm trees, while Thomas's 400 acres of plantation ranked as the second largest such area in the East Riding in 1812.

The walks in the grounds of Welton Hall and the plantations on the Wold and along Welton Dale became popular places of excursion in the early nineteenth century. 'Respectable persons' were permitted into the 'Welton Walks' being provided with a key to the various gates 'on entering their names in a book kept for that purpose at the lodge'. The Revd. James Allen described part of the Lower Walk in 1841 as follows:

> *All along on the left hand in a semicircle, is a neat shrubbery, in which are planted persian lilac, lauristinus, purple lilac, laurel, french currant bushes, wild cherry, laburnum, mock-orange, holly, viburnum, bladder-knot, white-spine, &c. Here is a neat temple, painted green, with fluted pillars, and surmounted with a chinese top....Proceeding along the path, which is a grass walk, in some places twenty feet wide, there stands in the middle of the way a noble beech tree of ten feet girth.*

The grounds of Welton Hall are now largely built upon but the street named Temple Walk keeps alive the position of the Lower Walk.

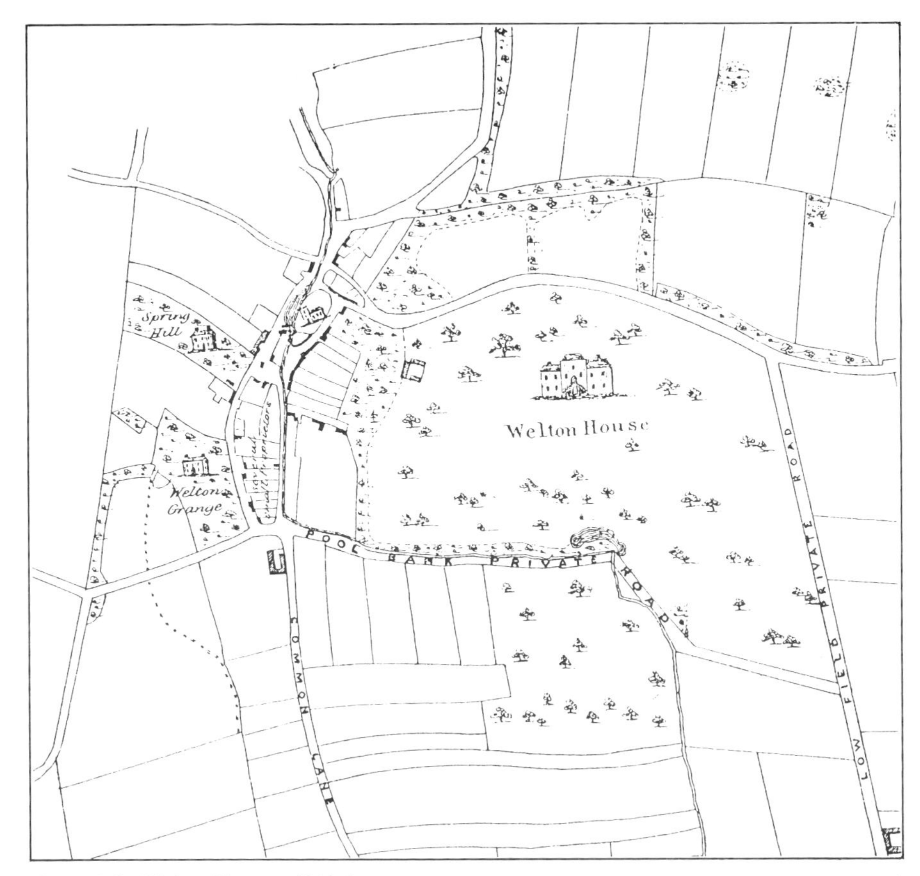

Part of the Welton Estate c.*1840* (*reproduced by permission of Hull University Archivist, Brynmor Jones Library*)

[Plan HCAO; D. Neave and E. Waterson, *Lost Houses of East Yorkshire*, 1988, pp.62-5; J. Allen, *The Stranger's Guide to Ferriby, Welton, Elloughton and South Cave*, 1841, pp.32-39]

BIOGRAPHICAL APPENDIX:

EIGHTEENTH CENTURY LANDSCAPE DESIGNERS WHO WORKED IN THE EAST RIDING OF YORKSHIRE

BRIDGEMAN, Charles (*c.*1680-1738)

Bridgeman collaborated from 1713 onwards with the architects, Sir John Vanbrugh, James Gibbs and William Kent and thus was in the forefront of progressive ideas of the time. In 1715 he came into his own as the leading professional in the transitional period of garden design between the geometric layouts of the late seventeenth century and early eighteenth century and the freer designs of Kent and Brown. His designs still included formal features — parterres, avenues, geometrical lakes and ponds — however with the introduction of garden buildings, statues, irregular shrubberies, rides and walks a transitional move towards the natural occurred.

In 1728 Bridgeman succeeded Henry Wise as Royal Gardener to George II and Queen Caroline and being in charge of the Royal Parks was responsible for the Round Pond and Serpentine in Kensington Gardens.

His major work was at Stowe, Buckinghamshire, seat of the 1st Viscount Cobham, where Bridgeman incorporated many of his progressive ideas. His plans for Scampston were produced in 1730 at about the same time as designs for Ledston in North Yorkshire.

Bridgeman is credited with the introduction into England from France of the 'ha-ha', the 'capital stroke, the leading step to all that has followed'. [Walpole]

(Peter Willis, *Charles Bridgeman and the English Landscape Garden*, Zwemmer, London, 1977)

BROWN, Lancelot (1716-1783)

Generally known as 'Capability' Brown, he was born in Northumberland and from *c.*1732-9 was employed by Sir William Loraine of Kirkharle Tower. In 1741 he became head gardener to Lord Cobham at Stowe, carrying out many of William Kent's designs. From the mid 1740s Brown took on independent commissions and he soon became the leading designer and practitioner in the natural style of landscape gardening, dominating the profession for some 35 years. Well over 200 commissions can be credited to Brown including such prestigious ones as those at Blenheim, Chatsworth and Petworth.

In 1764 he was appointed Master Gardener at Hampton Court where he planted the Great Vine which still flourishes. His huge practice required the employment of several foremen to oversee his commissions and amongst them were THOMAS WHITE and ADAM MICKLE.

Amongst Brown's Yorkshire commissions were Harewood House and Temple Newsam and the laying out of five grounds in the East Riding at BURTON CONSTABLE, HOWSHAM, RISE, SCAMPSTON and SLEDMERE.

Brown left no published material on his work, but in a letter of 1775 expressed his views on the essential requirements for a successful landscape designer:

> *a perfect knowledge of the country and the objects in it, whether natural or artificial, and infinite delicacy in the planting, etc. so much Beauty depending on the size of the trees and the colour of the leaves to produce the effect of light and shade.*

(Dorothy Stroud, *Capability Brown*, Faber & Faber, London, 1975)

EMES, William (1730-1803)

Active 1760-1800. There is no evidence that Emes was ever a pupil of Capability Brown, however he worked in a very similar style. Head gardener at Kedleston Hall, Derbyshire in 1756 he set up as an independent designer *c.*1760. By 1770 he was living near Derby, he later moved to Hampshire and died in London. Over 65 commissions by Emes have been identified including Belton House, Lincolnshire, Calke Abbey, Derbyshire, Powis Castle, Wales and Keele Park, Staffordshire. he worked mainly in the north Midlands and in north Wales for a great range of clients on estates ranging in size from a few acres to extensive parks. He had a reputation for the creation of cascades and lakes. The landscaping at CAVE CASTLE (1787) was his most northerly commission.

(Information from Dr. Keith Goodway, Keele University)

KNOWLTON, THOMAS (1691-1781)

Born at Chislehurst, Kent, in 1691 Thomas Knowlton was working as a gardener in Hertfordshire by 1711. In the years 1720-25 he was gardener to James Sherard, a London apothecary, who established at Eltham in Kent one of the most famous collections of rare and exotic plants. Here Knowlton would have been introduced to the cultivation of coffee, papaws, and pineapples. After leaving Sherard's service 'in a huff' Knowlton became for a short time head gardener to James Brydges, Duke of Chandos, at Canons, Middlesex, which was then one of the grandest houses in England. After Canons, Knowlton was briefly at Petworth House and Buckingham House before being appointed gardener at Londesborough by the end of 1726. Although bemoaning its distance from London Knowlton was happy at Londesborough and remained there until his death at the age of ninety in 1781. On Londesborough passing to the Dukes of Devonshire after the death of Lord Burlington in 1753, Knowlton also worked at Chatsworth being appointed 'director of his Grace's new kitchen garden, stoves, &c.' Part of Knowlton's income came from nursery gardens which he appears to have established in Walkergate, Beverley from 1737 and Sculcoates, Hull from 1752.

Knowlton was an indefatigable collector of plants — both cultivated and wild. He visited Holland on at least three occasions and also went to Guernsey in search of new plants. He corresponded with numerous botanists and antiquarians throughout Britain and on the Continent. In East Yorkshire his contacts included Dr. William Chambers of Hull (d.1785) whom he had first met at Leyden in 1726, and John Grimston of Kilnwick-on-the-Wolds.

Knowlton is known to have advised on the gardens and landscaping at BIRDSALL, BURTON CONSTABLE, EVERINGHAM, and SOUTH DALTON in the East Riding, Aldby Park, Duncombe Park, and Swinton in the North Riding and Blyborough in Lincolnshire as well as carrying out the important changes to the grounds at LONDESBOROUGH itself. No actual design can be attributed to Knowlton.

Knowlton has been described as 'undoubtedly one of the most outstanding gardeners of his time' by Blanche Henrey whose splendid study *No ordinary gardener: Thomas Knowlton 1691-1781* (A. O. Chater ed.) was published posthumously by the British Museum (Natural History) in 1986.

MICKLE, Adam (d.1809)

Mickle, who came from Bedale, North Yorkshire was employed as a foreman or clerk of works by Capability Brown for over 20 years between April 1757 and August 1779. He and his son Adam, jnr., worked at Sandbeck, the South Yorkshire estate of the 4th earl of Scarbrough, 1771-5, overseeing the implementation of Brown's scheme for landscaping the adjacent Roche Abbey.

Mickle travelled widely and was said, by John Claudius Loudon, to be 'a good deal employed to lay out grounds in the north of England'. Plans exist for several Yorkshire estates including Sutton Park, Newby-on-Swale (Baldersby), Kippax Park, Harewood and the modest grounds at Walkington. From 1796 Mickle was employed on the picturesque improvements being carried out for William Danby at Swinton, North Riding. He died at Londonderry near Bedale in 1809.

WHITE, Thomas (1739-1811)

Born at Shifnal, Shropshire, the son of a farmer, White was employed by Capability Brown 1759-65. He acted as foreman for Brown at Chillington, Staffordshire, Sandbeck, South Yorkshire and Temple Newsam, near Leeds. His handsome survey map of Chillington dated 1761 indicates that he had received training as a surveyor. From 1765 White was employed by the Lascelles family at Harewood and Goldsborough and in 1768 by William Weddell at Newby near Ripon.

Following early commissions for landscape designs in the East Riding at BURTON CONSTABLE (1768), HOUGHTON HALL (1768) and WELTON (1769), White produced his first improvement plan for an estate in Scotland in 1770. This was for Archibald Douglas at Douglas Castle, Lanarkshire. Other notable Scottish contracts followed later including Scone Palace, Abercairny and Buchanan. He spent a large part of his working life visiting estates in England and Scotland on planting and landscaping contracts. He was joined by his son, Thomas jnr., in his later work. Later East Riding commissions included work at SLEDMERE (1776), HOLME-ON-SPALDING MOOR (1777) and GRIMSTON GARTH (1782) and also possibly at BIRDSALL (1775), KILNWICK-ON-THE WOLDS and Melbourne Hall (1793). If he did draw up an improvement plan for Melbourne Hall it would be White's latest known English landscape commission because otherwise he worked solely in Scotland after 1787. Over 100 commissions by White (including those on which his son was jointly or independently involved) have been identified and 66 of his attractive plans, in watercolour on paper mounted on linen, are known to exist.

By 1773 White and his family were living at West Retford, Nottinghamshire, where they remained until about 1799. In 1773 White had purchased an area of barren moorland at Butsfield, near Lanchester, County Durham and here he and his son created a flourishing, well-wooded estate which became known as 'Woodlands'. His skills as a tree planter were recognised with the award of 11 medals by the Society of Arts, London. White's interest in agricultural matters was wide-ranging and his enthusiastic advocation of the cultivation of the larch tree culminated in his request that his coffin should be made from the wood of the larch. His obituaries record his 'convivial and pleasing manners' and Sir Henry Steuart in *The Planters' Guide* of 1828 remarked:

> *Mr. White was an excellent agriculturist, an ingenious mechanic, and a planter of great skill. Like his master Brown, he was in the habit of undertaking the execution of his own designs, and also of plantations of considerable extent, in both England and Scotland, until his business as a Landscape Gardener, in the latter country, became too extensive to admit of such undertakings.*

By White's death in 1811 the fashion for the 'natural style' of landscape gardens had declined in favour of a rising interest in the picturesque and later a move back to a smaller scale formality.

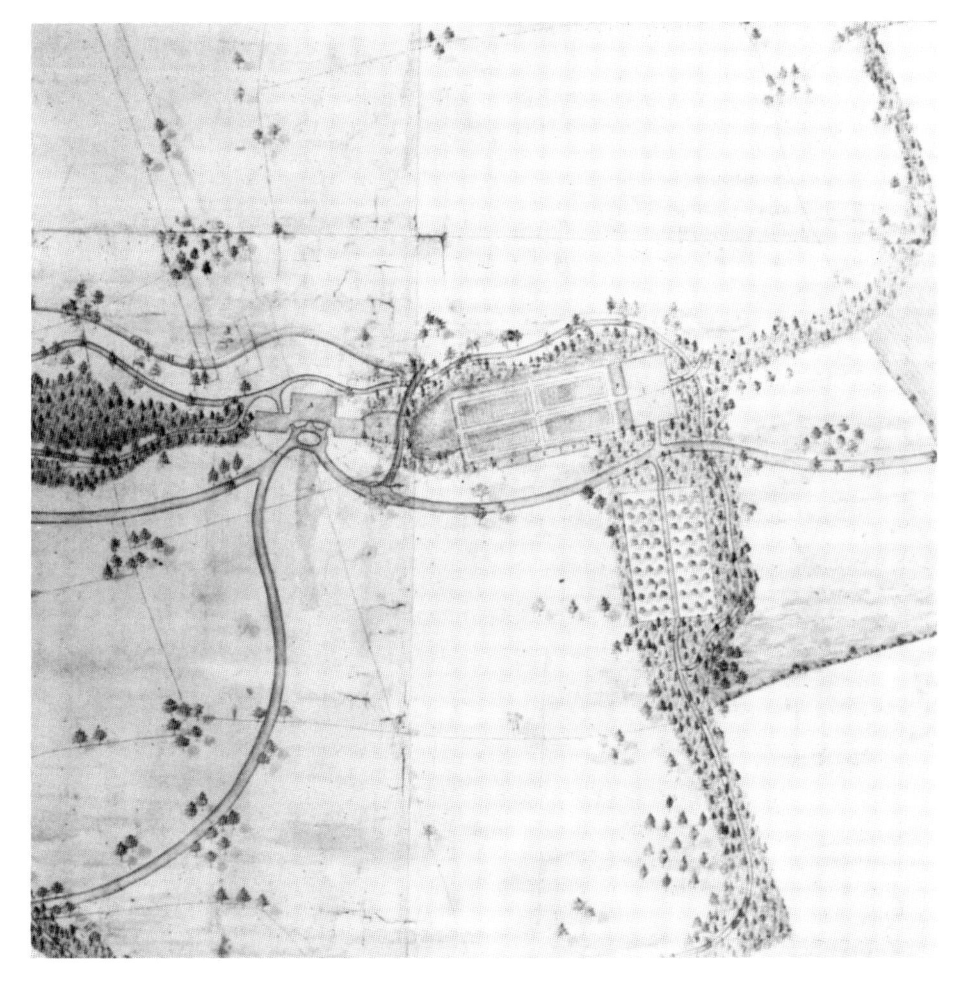

Houghton, detail of improvement plan by Thomas White, 1768, showing hall and kitchen garden
(Lord Manton/Hull University Photographic Service)

(D. K. M. Turnbull 'Thomas White (1739-1811): Eighteenth century Landscape Designer and Arboriculturist', unpublished Ph.D. thesis, University of Hull, 1990; D. Neave 'The Search for Thomas White — Landscape Gardener', *Georgian Society for East Yorkshire Newsletter*, 11, 1984; A. A. Tait *The Landscape Garden in Scotland 1735-1835*, Edinburgh University Press, 1980)

SELECT BIBLIOGRAPHY

K. J. Allison *The East Riding of Yorkshire Landscape*, London, 1976

B. Coates 'Park Landscapes of the East and West Ridings in the Time of Humphry Repton', *Yorkshire Archaeological Journal*, 41, pp.465-480

B. English *The Great Landowners of East Yorkshire 1530-1910*, Hemel Hempstead, 1990

A. Harris *The Rural Landscape of The East Riding of Yorkshire 1750-1850*, Oxford, 1961

B. Henrey *No Ordinary Gardener: Thomas Knowlton 1691-1781*, London, 1986

D. Jacques *Georgian Gardens*, London, 1983

S. Neave *Medieval Parks of East Yorkshire*, Hull, 1991

D. Neave and E. Waterson *Lost Houses of East Yorkshire*, Hull, 1988

G. Sheeran *Landscape Gardens in West Yorkshire*, Wakefield, 1990

D. Stroud *Capability Brown*, Faber and Faber, London, 1975

D. Turnbull 'Thomas White (1739-1811): Eighteenth century Landscape Designer and Arboriculturist', unpublished Ph.D. thesis, University of Hull, 1990

P. Willis *Charles Bridgeman and the English Landscape Garden*, London, 1977

M. Wilson *William Kent Architect, Designer, Painter, Gardener*, London, 1984

Abbreviations:

HCAO - Humberside County Archive Office

HUL - Hull University Library

The gardens at Scampston Hall c.1780. Watercolour by Francis Nicholson. (Hull University Photographic Service)

ACKNOWLEDGEMENTS

We are indebted to the following who have kindly allowed access to their grounds and in many cases assisted with information and illustrative material: Dr. and Mrs. R. Ashwin, R. A. Bethell, J. Chichester-Constable, J. P. Clappison, Lord and Lady Hotham, S. Knock, Mary, Lady Legard, Sir Charles and Lady Legard, Sir Ian and Lady Macdonald, Lord and Lady Manton, Richard Marriott, Oliver Marriott, Mr. and Mrs. S. Martin, Lord and Lady Middleton and Sir Tatton Sykes.

Illustrations and/or information have been generously provided by Dr. Barbara English, Peter Goodchild, Dr. Keith Goodway, Elisabeth Hall, Dr. John Harvey, Edward Ingram, Dr. Francis Johnson, Berna Moody, Jan Odey and A. R. B. Robinson. Permission to reproduce material has been kindly granted by Hull Museums and Art Galleries, Wakefield Library and Art Gallery, Leeds city Art Gallery (Burton Constable), Hull University Archivist, the Dean and Chapter of York, and the Bodleian Library, Oxford. Particular thanks to Humberside Archaeological Unit, especially Ed Dennison, and to Roland Wheeler-Osman of Hull University Photographic Service for photography.

We acknowledge the help received from the staff at Humberside County Archive Office, York Minster Library, the Local History libraries at Beverley and Hull, the Brynmor Jones Library, University of Hull and in particular archivist Brian Dyson, the archivists at Chatsworth House and the Yorkshire Archaeological Society and Dr. D. Connell at Burton Constable.

We are most grateful for the encouragement received for this project from Captain Angus Hildyard and other members of the executive committee of the Georgian Society for East Yorkshire. we have also received invaluable help at all stages from Dr. Susan Neave.

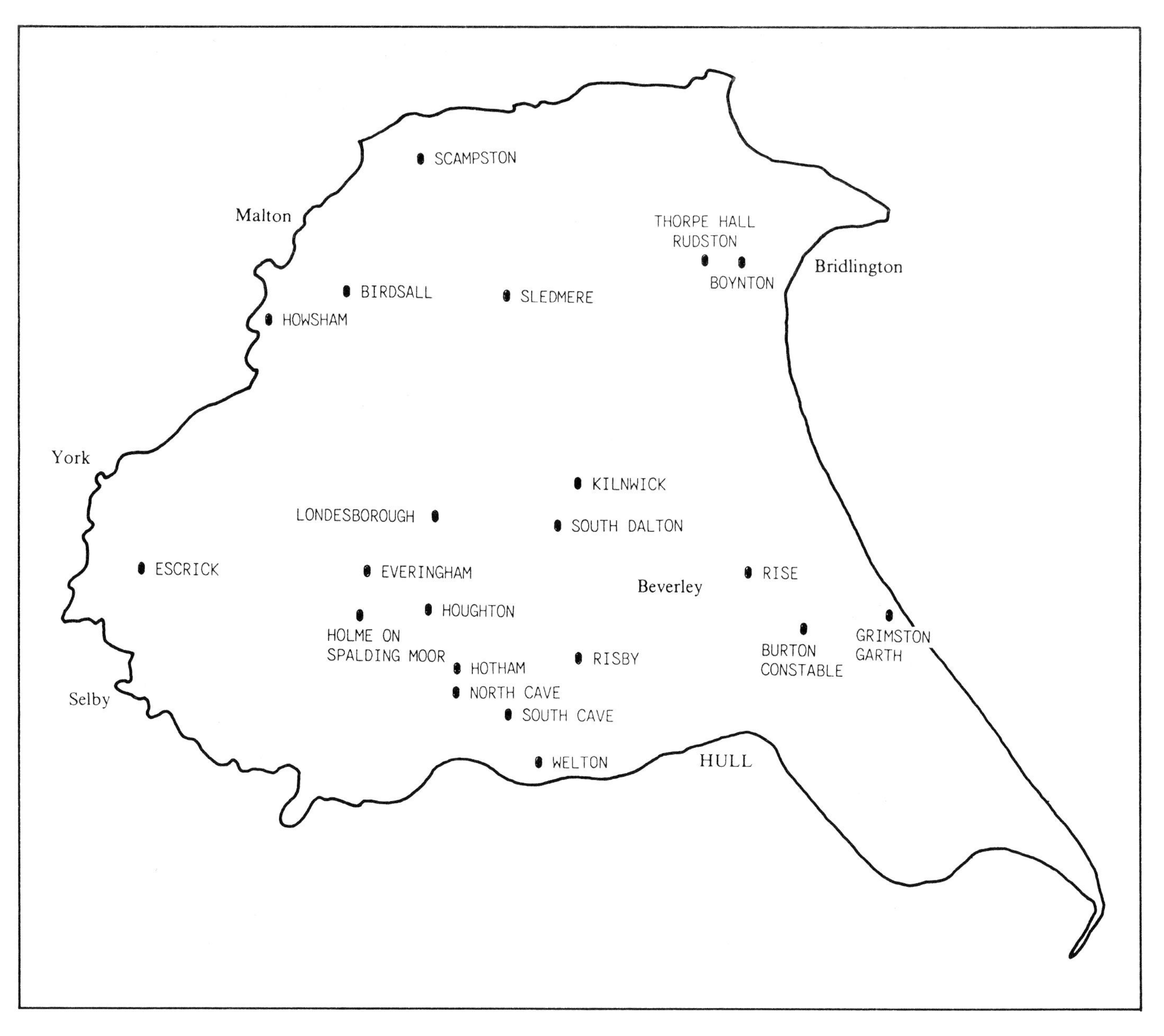

East Riding of Yorkshire. Location of landscaped parks and gardens described in gazetteer.

Birdsall. Looking south across the bottom lake to the modern temple. (*Hull University Photographic Service*)

Index of East Riding parks mentioned in text: Gazetteer entry in bold type.

Londesborough. Looking north-east from the cascade across the second lake. (Hull University Photographic Service)